...AND, THEN I CHOSE NOT TO DIE!

The Brighter Facets of Fears, Failures, & Fantasies

A Self Help Book By
Dr. Minakshi Sehrawat

BLUEROSE PUBLISHERS
U.K.

Copyright © Dr. Minakshi Sehrawat 2025

All rights reserved by author. No part of this publication may be reproduced, stored in a retrieval system or transmitted in any form or by any means, electronic, mechanical, photocopying, recording or otherwise, without the prior permission of the author. Although every precaution has been taken to verify the accuracy of the information contained herein, the publisher assumes no responsibility for any errors or omissions. No liability is assumed for damages that may result from the use of information contained within.

BlueRose Publishers takes no responsibility for any damages, losses, or liabilities that may arise from the use or misuse of the information, products, or services provided in this publication.

For permissions requests or inquiries regarding this publication, please contact:

BLUEROSE PUBLISHERS
www.BlueRoseONE.com
info@bluerosepublishers.com
+4407342408967

ISBN: 978-93-6783-487-9

Cover design: Daksh
Typesetting: Tanya Raj Upadhyay

First Edition: March 2025

…And, Then I Chose Not To Die!

The brighter facets of fears, failures, and fantasies

To all who stood by me on this journey, offering unwavering support and encouragement…
With profound gratitude, utmost respect, and heartfelt appreciation,
"Your guidance and support will forever be the light that illuminates my path."

PREFACE

There was a time when I hit the lowest low and darkest dark in life. I sat there, barely breathing, staring into a void that seemed endless. The clock ticked on, and I sat on that edge when any second could have registered for claiming my life. Just one step away from letting the pain consume me entirely, I was exhausted by those 'fears' and 'failures' of life.

For a fleeting moment, I firmly closed my eyes. My exhausted mind took me to a world of fantasies, a place where I felt seen, fearless, free, and alive. In this world, there were waves of laughter, possibilities, acknowledgment, appreciation, and a sense of belonging. For unknown reasons, I felt an undeniable pull toward this world. I wanted to create this world, live in it, and be worthy of everything beyond disgrace and despair.

Amid too noisy silence, I opened my eyes and told myself - to do better, be better, be worthy of 'new beginnings', and 'new possibilities' and 'new life'.

Hey, my name is Minakshi Sehrawat, and this book is a reflection of the lessons, insights and experiences that shaped my life ever after. It's not just a book—it's about the mind-sets, shifting thoughts, self-discoveries and actions that can probably help you reclaim your life beyond facts, fears and failures.

"There was a time when I felt my pain and heartbreak were unique, as if no one else could possibly understand the depth of what I was going through. It felt isolating, as if the world around me couldn't comprehend the weight I carried. But then, I found solace in books and conversations. I turned to people, stories and poems that spoke to my very soul, shared by people who had walked through similar storms. Their words echoed my emotions—my anguish, my love, my confusion—and reminded me that my struggles were not solitary. They were part of a shared human experience, woven into the same fabric of life that connects us all. Through their voices, I discovered comfort, understanding, and a strength I didn't know I had. It was as if those storytellers whispered, "You're not alone; we're here too.""

CONTENTS

CHAPTER 1
THE POWER OF PROBABILITY 1
- The Power of Trying 4
- I Chose Being. I Chose Life. 10
- Baby Steps of a Writer 13
- When Cruelty of Life Gives Birth to Good 16
- And, A Writer Forever 21

CHAPTER 2
FEAR, INSECURITIES, AND ADVANTAGE 25
- Insecurities Drive Fear 28
- Fear Attracts Too 30
- Fear Owned Me a Space 33
- Fear of Unknown 35
- Fear of Getting Replaced 37
- Love and Fear Paradox 40

CHAPTER 3
SOLITUDE IS NOT THAT BAD 44
- If You Don't Know Solitude, You Don't Know Freedom 48
- Joy of Solo Escapes 50
- Together and Alone - Solitude in Groups 52
- Abysses of Solitude 55
- Self-Space Has Boundaries 57
- Parenthood and Boundaries 62
- Boundaries and Self-Esteem –Intertwined 65

CHAPTER 4
THAT PRESSURE OF BEING HAPPY 67
- Constant Happiness is Deception 69

Happiness Vs Pleasure 71
　　Chasing Happiness is a Trap 75
　　Horizons of Happiness 76

CHAPTER 5
THE SCIENCE BEHIND CHOOSING VALUES 91
　　We Do Both - Chose and Chase - Values 96
　　Protecting Values or Taking a U-turn 100
　　Authentic or In-Authentic Self and Values 105
　　Values in Tumultuous Relationships 108
　　Values in Leadership Role 109
　　Finally, the Collective Wisdom 112

CHAPTER 6
THE HYPES AROUND PERFECTION—
REAL OR SHALLOW? 114
　　Hype Kills Your Story 119
　　Hype Vs Play-down 121
　　Imperfection is OK 126
　　Realism and Perfection 128
　　Perception Is 'Not Always' a Reality 130

CHAPTER 7
I WANT SUCCESS BUT SUCCESS DOESN'T
WANT ME 135
　　The Hollow Pursuit of Success: Nick's Story 136
　　Failure Is Truly Essential 139
　　Choose Struggle, Not Just Success 142
　　Roads and Destination of Elusive Success 144
　　Self-Reflection on 'Close but Not Quite'
　　　　Stances 147
　　And, Afterwards, I Was No More the Same
　　　　Girl 150

CHAPTER 8
MINIMALISM AND MARKETING OF EMOTIONS 157
    The Power of 'Less' 160
    Simple Living Philosophies across Cultures 164
    Emotional Pull vs. Minimalist Calm 167
    Navigating Emotional Triggers 170
    Dealing with Emotional Traps 173
    We've Come A Full Circle 175
    Finding Balance 177

CHAPTER 9
THE UNEXPLORED DARK UNIVERSE INSIDE 179
    Who Am I? 180
    The Unseen Us 183
    Still Here, Still Exploring 184
    One Step at a Time 187
    …And, Then I Chose Not To Die! 191

CHAPTER 1
THE POWER OF PROBABILITY

Chapter 1
The Power of Probability

On the window seat of a Vistara flight from Mumbai to Delhi, I sat gazing out of the window. The city was looking like a patchwork of lights and shadows as the plane climbed higher. My mind wandered to the session I had just delivered at a reputed university—an invited guest session that felt both rewarding and fulfilling. I recalled the luxurious stay, the delicious meals, and the energy of the day. Now, as I headed home, a sense of quiet contentment washed over me.

After some time, lulled by the steady hum of the engines, I moved slowly into a light nap. In that brief-moment, I had a dream—a vivid reel of memories from my life. Scenes from my childhood, the carefree laughter of school days, and the excitement of college life flashed by. Then came the bittersweet memory of the love from yesterday, followed by the overwhelming joy of my child's birth. The dream moved on to the challenges I had faced, the struggles that tested me, and the comebacks that redefined me. It felt like a condensed recap of three decades, playing out in the span of a few minutes.

I woke up to the soft voice of the air hostess, gently asking, "Tea or coffee?" Still half-immersed in the dream, I replied, "Hot water." I glanced out of the window again. The clouds outside stretched endlessly, appearing like white butter and soft feathers against the blue sky. Sitting above them, I felt an odd sense of clarity and peace.

As I watched those clouds, a thought sparked in my mind. Life changes its course in ways we never expect. It breaks us, remoulds us, and sometimes, gives us the space to become something we never know. Inspired by the moment, I pulled out a piece of paper and a pencil from my bag. Being a writer, I've always cherished preserving thoughts before they get lost in the noise of a hundred others.

And so, from there, the journey began. Right there, thousands of feet above the ground, with the clouds as my witness, the idea of writing a self-help book took shape. What I jotted down on that paper were the beginnings of something bigger—the points that would eventually become the chapters of a book. Each point held a piece of my life, a lesson learned, or a story worth telling. It felt personal, raw, and meaningful. It felt as though the book was already forming in my mind, waiting to be written—not just for myself but for those who might find a part of their story in mine. Perhaps, through those chapters, someone might find comfort, hope, or even a reason to keep moving forward.

As the flight continued, I sat there, above the clouds, holding on to the thought. Life has a way of inspiring us when we least expect it, isn't it?

The Power of Trying

"Trying doesn't guarantee a win, but not trying certainly guarantees a loss"

The first and most powerful thought that came to me was about the power of trying—the power of probability. In mathematical terms, probability is the possibility of a certain desirable outcome. Imagine that in any situation, you can either win or lose. Here, the probability of both winning and losing is one-half—two outcomes, each with equal chances.

When you understand probability, you understand the value of efforts. It reminds you that the chance of winning still exists, no matter how slim it may seem. Yes, failure can also occur, but the important thing is that there's still a chance.

If you're alive to see another sunrise, it means you still have opportunities left. It means God hasn't closed the door on you, your abilities, or the probabilities that life holds. During my darkest moments, I clung to this belief. I made one thing certain that I would never stop trying.

And you know what? That persistence opened-up new horizons for me—opportunities I couldn't have imagined. It added diversity and depth to my life. I've learned that trying doesn't guarantee a win, but not trying certainly guarantees a loss.

Life, like probability, gives us chances—sometimes we win, sometimes we lose. What matters is the effort we put in. With each attempt, we shape our own probability, and the more we try, the greater our chances of success become.

"Life is a school of Probability." – Walter

It was a cool evening in December 2017. After dinner, I went for my usual walk with my mother, just like every other day. We talked about the little things—how my day had been, what I had accomplished, and then moved on to our plans, thoughts, and health. Our conversation spanned everything from the past to the present and even the future. Like always our talk would conclude with her assertions that I should keep faith alive, should keep working hard and shouldn't worry much. She would assure me that 'everything will be soon alright and you will have a better tomorrow'.

My all-weather friend, my mom is a very simple, well-educated, and a soft-spoken lady, perfectly groomed and cultured in North Indian Society. She would listen to my daily routine things, give her viewpoint on them, and then would conclude every day talk with a hope, a belief and a relief. She would attest our trust in the almighty, for He would listen to all prayers and that the answers come in time. But what were those prayers? What was I looking forward to? Well, to understand that, I need to share a few episodes of my story and reflect on how the power of trying or probability works in our life—something like—when you feel all odds are against you, and yet, somehow, something shifts, and you get those unexpected chances.

In those times, under overwhelmed pressing circumstances, I was in a dire need of a job. A job for breathing, living, and surviving. In those days, I was a broken woman, caught between the ruins of a painful separation, grief, and a constant sense of fear and uncertainty. I had just lost everything—my family, my career, and the life I had once known. All that was left was a heart full of sorrow and a mind exhausted by heartache. My personal life had crumbled, and professionally, I had no job to hold onto. Yet, amid this darkness, I had one precious responsibility of raising the then 4-year-old son- my only reason to wake up each morning!

Alone me, was stripped of all the support systems and left to figure out how to survive. To me, the things to begin with were—barely the clothes on my back, the worn-out shoes on my feet, and the small, fragile child who clung to me for comfort. My bank balance reflected my dire situation—just INR 3245, to die or to live. Yes, but I had my parents to go to who would not just rescue me but would also nurture me the way they did when I was a small girl and help me rebuild my broken world.

Well, among death and life, I had to choose. Believe me, death appeared to be a real reliever to me from all those immense pains and sufferings that tore you apart-not just once but with each second, each minute, and each interval of the day. Constant flow or those horrible thoughts, and those haunting memories of a life (close to a death) had wrenched my psyche and nothing under the sky could help to restore my hopes back in life. You are just alive because you are breathing, your eyes are blinking, your heart is plumbing and your body movements are intact. Rest, you are dead by all other means. This means that you are resting in peace while not actually resting in peace. No dose of motivation can work on you, no inspirational talk would go beyond my ear drums. Those days have taught me some real and significant life lessons that otherwise, are never taught in any school, college, or university. No teacher on the earth could dare to teach them.

Personally and professionally broken I could now figure out the difference between '*jinda hona*' and '*jinda rehna*'. But you can't cook even a day's meal by blending your emotions and shedding tears. They would not waive your bills off. You are not going to get a concession on a price tag just because you are broken and trust me, people are not at all interested in listening to your story of grief either.

I witnessed the changing times, changing circumstances, and then, changing voice tones. Well, I am not here to worry about being judged—by society or anyone else. That was never my fight. My fight then was about survival to figure out what comes next. How will I make it through? What will I do? Where will I live? How will I earn?

"Take all the time you need to wade, sleep late, rage, or curse whichever deity works best for you. You've been victimized, and for a strong, smart woman—and you're both—that's as devastating as it is frustrating. When you're done, you'll figure out what to do next."

Confidence? I didn't even have a shred of self-belief. Those were days of trauma that thrust me into a peculiar silence. But this wasn't the peaceful silence of serenity; it was a deafening roar inside my head and heart. To the outside world, I seemed calm, almost stoic, but internally, I was unravelling. Writing became my solace. Expressing my heart out on scraps of paper gave me a temporary relief, though those moments were fleeting. Many times, my words were dispersed with ink as my tears soaked the pages. Most of those pieces were torn to shreds and discarded, as if I could throw my pain into the bin alongside them. But pain is not so easily disposed of. Even after a year, nothing seemed to change. I wasn't better—not even by a fraction. The grief held on, stubborn and unyielding. Those who saw me might have thought I was 'managing' but deep down, I knew I wasn't healed. It wasn't just about surviving anymore; it was about figuring out how to transform the chaos within into something meaningful. And yet, at that time, I couldn't see the way forward. The pain felt eternal, like a shadow that clung to me even when the sun was nowhere in sight.

"To be on the earth is to know- the restlessness of remaining a seed, the pain of being planted, the struggle with the sunlight, the joy of bearing fruits, the dispersing of seeds, the decaying of seasons, and eventually the mystery of life and death."

An intricate web of overwhelming emotions, fears, and responsibilities can make you feel all-encompassing, self-questioning, wondering if I wasn't enough, replaying past moments to understand where things went wrong. And, it's not just about losing a partner but also the shared dreams and security that once existed. What amplified my vulnerability was, that I was unemployed and financially insecure. Though my maternal instincts drove me to stay strong, the weight of responsibility is crushing, with anxiety and stress. Inwardly, I often oscillated between despair and resilience. Walk, crawl, or creep, I determined not to stop moving to take myself out of those wild storms. On some days, the grief would paralyze me, while on others, I gathered every ounce of strength to look for solutions—whether it was applying for jobs, seeking support, or simply holding it together.

At a snail's pace, I began taking small steps forward. Be it through leaning on loved ones, rediscovering my talents, or simply allowing myself to grieve, I was trying things. This process, though arduous, had planted the seeds of a new beginning, new tries, and new trust. It was not just about surviving—it was about learning to rebuild a life, not just for myself but for the little soul who was dependent on me. There is a saying that when a caterpillar realizes that the world is over, it becomes a butterfly! Holding onto that fragile hope, I convinced myself not to give up—not just yet. I must get up, and go on even if with wounded and bleeding feet. Instead of giving in, I decided to give myself three months.

I Chose Being. I Chose Life.

Amid the life and the death, I chose to stay alive for three more months, to see what would unfold in my story. Each day, I convinced myself not to give in, with reasons—real or imagined—just to keep going. Coincidentally, those months led up to an exam I'd registered for almost a year earlier. My parents kept encouraging me to study, telling me I could do it, trying to build my confidence. But deep down, I wasn't so sure.

I decided not to give up, reasoning, *"I can always die later if I have to, but for now - let's see if the story takes a turn."*

After taking the exam and getting through those three months, I felt a little calm, and that urge to give up also became just a tiny fraction less. With barely any hope but a dim spark of determination, I began taking small, hesitant steps forward. I started applying for jobs at local schools and colleges, unsure of what lay ahead but willing to see where the next chapter might lead.

Each rejection at interviews stung like salt on an open wound. I, who once dared to appear for tough competitive exams, was now struggling to secure even an entry-level teaching job.

My confidence felt as low as that of someone starting out for the very first time, and it felt like the world could see my fears. But as crushing as it was, I kept showing up—sometimes with trembling hands and other times with a faint spark of hope. Every step I took was a revolt against the despair threatening to pull me under. My belief in the possibility of a better tomorrow—however distant—became a reason for continuing.

Over time, I withdrew into myself completely, speaking rarely and finding solace in the dark corners of my room. The light, both literal and figurative, felt unbearable. My parents became my pillars of strength, and my little son, my only source of joy. My family tried to support me however they could, and my sister-in-law eventually helped me secure a small job at a local college. With the college bus as my commute, I began this new chapter with just three sets of clothes and a modest pair of sandals. At first, the small acts of moving forward brought moments of happiness, but they also brought an overwhelming sadness. Every time I felt a tiny joy, I was consumed by guilt, convincing myself I didn't deserve it. I can tell you that whenever any action makes me happy, I'll become sadder the next moment. I would cry more and tell myself that I don't deserve the happiness. The shadow, and protection my father provided shielded me from much of life's harshness. His wise words, shaped by a lifetime of experiences, restored my confidence, and he made sure to connect with me every day, offering guidance and reassurance.

As the days passed, I began to notice the smallest of changes in myself. The routine of waking up, getting ready, and catching the bus became a lifeline—something to hold onto in the chaos of my emotions. My son's laughter after school, the way he hugged me when I got home, reminded me of why I was doing this. Some days were harder than others; there were moments when I barely had the strength to leave my bed. But every time I saw his face light up when I walked through the door, it gave me a reason to keep moving forward.

After a month at my job, I began talking to a colleague, sharing small pieces of myself. It was then I realized I wasn't entirely invisible. One day, I bought a notebook and started jotting down small victories—a kind word from a co-worker, my son's school project, or even just making it through a tough day. Those notes became a quiet reminder that even when I felt lost, I was still moving forward, one step at a time.

With time, life did get better, but the progress was painfully slow. Three months into my first job, I came across an opportunity for a short-term writing position at an IT company in a big city. I decided to move, though the thought of leaving my parents' home for a job in another city filled me with apprehension, especially when my emotional health was still fragile. From that point on, I had to manage everything on my own. Encouraged strongly by my parents, I packed my bag with just 4–5 pairs of winter clothes and left my hometown in tears. I remember how my mother spent long hours counselling me, helping me navigate this difficult transition. Thankfully, that IT Company was going to provide me with accommodation and meals for the first two weeks, giving me some time to find a more permanent place.

Baby Steps of a Writer

That small two-month contract job as a content writer turned out to be an unintentional training ground, a crash course in the basics of professional writing. It was there that I first learned how to structure ideas, meet deadlines, and write with the readers in mind. I struggled at first, often doubting if I was any good at it. But with every piece I wrote, I discovered something new about my capabilities. It wasn't just about writing—it was about realizing that I could adapt and learn, even in the most challenging circumstances. Those small appreciations and acknowledgements among the teammates had uplifted a bit of my confidence, and I have a little pint of joys too during meal time conversations. That short stint planted the seed of self-reliance and gave me the confidence to pursue writing further. Though it was temporary and far from ideal, it laid the foundation and honed the 'writing skills' that would stay with me till I die.

It wasn't just a job—it was a stepping stone in rebuilding things further. Knowing that I can't keep all my axes in one box, I also discovered ways to work on freelance writing projects. Surprisingly, it was merely for INR 70, then 120 and then 500 to start with. But I came out believing that I was capable of something more, that I could stand on my own two feet again.

After a brief period of two months, this contractual job ended, and I found myself looking for another job. Now, this third job came to me after a month, with a low salary, gruelling work targets, and a hostile work environment. What made it worse was that I had no stable place to live this time. I was temporarily staying with a female friend; someone I had once supported during her difficult times. Ironically, in my moment of need, her hospitality was limited, and I found myself walking on eggshells in her home.

"I still vividly remember one particularly cold night. When after returning from my exhausting 8-to-6 job, I pushed myself to work on a freelance writing project to make ends meet. By 2 a.m., I had finished the work, but the mental toll left me starving. Yet, accessing the kitchen was not an option—it was off-limits. As I lay in bed, stomach growling, I suddenly recalled that my mom had packed three parathas for me when I left my hometown on Monday morning. By some miracle, I

discovered one still in my bag. Though slightly stale and edged with fungus, it was a taste of home and love. Tears streamed down my face as I ate it, grateful for the comfort it brought. That simple paratha, infused with my mother's care, was enough to lull me to sleep that night and face the next day."

Moving forward, I continued this third job for merely 2 weeks. What followed was a life-altering episode that marked the beginning of an unexpected turning point in my journey. To be true, it was hard for me to continue that job because neither the job was good nor did I have any place to live. Moreover, the locality of that office was the area where I used to hang around with the love of my life in our golden days. Now, whenever I look towards those hills visible from the office window, I recall those beautiful memories of the old days and would get lost in those times but return wrenched. We can't undo the past, we can only learn to live with it, somehow peacefully. But I was not at all at peace. Between the past, present, and future, I was stuck. My past was not ready to leave me, my present was horrible and my future was blurred.

Adding another pain, my father was diagnosed with cancer, and the toll it took on me was immense. He began chemotherapy, and my desire to leave my job and be with my family grew stronger each day. I wanted to offer my physical and emotional support, help with his treatment, and just be there for them in any way I could. But my parents, ever the pillars of strength, insisted that

I stay at my job, reassuring me that I would eventually adjust to the situation. Despite their encouragement, my heart wasn't in it.

I felt torn between two worlds—one where my family needed me and another where I had to continue working just to survive. The emotional and physical toll of wanting to be in two places at once, trying to be present for both my job and my parents, left me exhausted and drained. My thoughts were consumed by my father's battle, and yet, I couldn't bring myself to let go of what was holding me in that job. The guilt, the responsibility, the love—it was a whirlwind of emotions I couldn't untangle.

When Cruelty of Life Gives Birth to Good

On the bright morning of March 2018, and like any other day, I started my commute to work, a tiring one-hour journey involving buses and autos. I arrived at the office, put my bag down, and asked the assistant for a coffee. Then, I stepped away briefly to freshen up, washing my face and looking into the mirror, and found myself lost in thoughts. As I stood there, something within me quietly asked, "Do you want to continue this job?" To my surprise, I found myself hesitantly answering, "No." But the other part of me, the rational part, pressingly asked again, "But you have no other means of survival, is that still your choice?" Despite the logic, I again found myself saying, "Yes."

It was as if I were having an internal debate, two parts of me battling for control. Finally, the decision was made. I grabbed my bag, walked out of the office without saying a word to anyone, and stepped into the unknown. The weight of the decision settled in as I walked away, but once I was far enough, I couldn't hold it in anymore. I broke down—running until exhaustion took over, I found myself leaning against a tree, sobbing uncontrollably, and feeling like I had lost everything. I cried like I had never cried before while hugging a tree, completely consumed by the gravity of my own actions. I remember a couple of boys from a nearby hostel came out to check if I needed help, but I could barely answer through my tears.

"She was tired, her back was aching, and her life too."- Jill Mansell

It took me a moment to gather myself. I splashed some water from my bottle on my face and took deep breaths, trying to ease the heaviness in my chest. Standing there by the traffic circle, I stared at the arrows pointing in different directions—East, West, North, and South. It all felt the same. I had no idea which way to go. Lost in my thoughts, I dialled my ex's number, desperately hoping to hear something comforting, but instead, I was met with cold & harsh words. The call got ended, making me feel even emptier than before.

What now? I thought. Without any clear direction, I took an auto-rickshaw to the place, where my bags and belongings were left. Remember that not-so-friendly friend? At her place, my belongings were kept. Well, I was in an auto and suddenly my phone rang up. It was an unknown number, and thinking that it must be from the workplace that I just left, I was reluctant to pick up. But after the second ring, I picked it up, still expecting it to be from the office. The voice on the other end, though, was completely unexpected. "Hey, I'm Varun calling. Is this Ms. Minakshi?" the voice asked. I took a breath, my heart racing. "Yes, please go ahead," I replied, unsure of what to expect next.

When I picked up that call from Varun, I had no idea that my life was going to offer me — a chance, a new beginning, once again. Just half an hour before, I walked out of my job, feeling like I had nothing left, and here was this voice, calm and sure, offering me something I didn't expect. "Ma'am, you've been selected," Varun said, and for a second, I couldn't even process the words. It felt like a dream. The job I had interviewed for months ago had somehow come back to me, and they were ready to offer me everything I needed—an accommodation, a position, and a future.

I could hardly believe it. I had been so consumed with feelings of hopelessness, trying to hold everything together, but after that moment everything shifted. I could finally breathe again, knowing there was a way forward. "Yes, sir, I'll be there," I said, my voice barely audible, trembling with gratitude and disbelief.

That call felt like the universe was reaching out to pull me out of the darkness. It wasn't just a job offer—it was a sign that there was more ahead for me, that my story wasn't over. It was as if the universe had been waiting for me to make that decision, to choose to keep going, and when I did, the path opened-up. My life, which had felt so uncertain, suddenly had a direction again.

Well, this was how I landed a job that would last for more than two years till Covid in 2020. Behind getting this job, there were dozens of interviews that I gave within a 200 to 250 Km radius of my hometown. To keep the expenses low, I used the cheapest transport I could find and walked whenever I could— to save money. When I was away from home, I even stood in line for free food packets just to get by. I never once thought of buying anything unnecessary—every penny mattered—for survival and sustenance.

Those days were tough, but they taught me how to keep going no matter what. Even when the probability of getting a job was the least, I appeared for the interview. You know that scientists experiment even when the probability of success is merely 0.00001 percent because the important thing is to take your chance when you can take it.

Alongside, I enrolled in a doctorate program to further my education. Both my son and I were studying at the same time. My father initially supported my studies until I could manage the expenses on my own.

Eventually, I earned the "Dr." prefix too, a symbol of the hard work and dedication it took to reach that milestone.

Abraham Maslow beautifully articulated in his 'Hierarchy of Needs' theory that a human's need range from the basic necessities that sustain life to the higher aspirations that give it meaning and purpose. At that time, I was living at the very base of this pyramid, where each day was a quest to meet these fundamental needs, and everything else felt like a distant dream. A breakthrough came with a job at a reputed college that provided in-campus accommodation in the Girl's Hostel with all basic furniture, all-time meals, and no need for transport since everything was within reach. They even allowed my 5-year-old son to stay with me. For the first time in a while, we had space, security, peace, and all the essentials. I couldn't help but feel God's kindness in those moments. Everything started to work out when I had almost no hope left. That's how life is—it surprises you when you least expect it. It taught you to accept and embrace uncertainties and to believe in the power of possibilities. Sometimes, even in the darkest moments.

"I am enough. My heart, my thoughts, and the stories that swirl in my mind are enough. I feel alive, full of energy, like I'm bubbling over with life. My early-morning walks, late-night baths, and even my loud laugh—it's all enough. My little quirks, like my whistle and my singing in the shower, are enough too. I'm like

a freshly poured pint, full of life. I am my own world, my own universe, with all its highs and lows. And if this is all there is—just me, nature, and the world around me—I've come to realize that it's more than enough."

And, A Writer Forever

This job would eventually become a launch pad for me to further discover my potential as a writer, anchor, and eventually an entrepreneur. With almost no time required for travel or cooking, I had space for creativity. It not only filled my evenings but also added to my income. I began accepting a lot of freelancing work assignments. I remember hardly saying no to any work and rarely missing a deadline. To my surprise, I explored various writing opportunities and completed 450 projects, both large and small, across industries like education, healthcare, IT, pharmaceuticals, HR services, politics, retail, sports, travel, the corporate sector, and NGOs. I also connected with a wide range of professionals, including industry experts, social and political leaders, and peers like designers and developers.

My identity as a writer grew alongside my teaching career, and I became known among people I had never met. Through word of mouth, appreciation for my work spread, bringing in even more opportunities. My weekends and evenings were no longer empty. While the desire for love and social connections still lingered, I found peace in being able to earn enough to live independently, pay my bills, and maintain my dignity. It was incredibly fulfilling to see my words turn into punchlines, campaign titles, billboards, business brochures, website content, articles, white papers, blogs, pitch decks, and even coffee table books. The highlights were when the speeches I wrote were delivered by Vice-Chancellors, and two of my articles were published in Forbes Magazine! This journey not only expanded my knowledge of the world but also brought financial rewards—sometimes in rupees, sometimes in dollars!

An Anchor too- One day, after a conversation at home, I decided to take a few days off for a family event. As I thought about it, I wondered if I could write for the organization behind the event, given my interest in their ideology. Without thinking too much, I sent them an email at 6:00 am, offering my services as an English writer. To my surprise, they called later that day, liked my sample, and offered me all their English writing work, which brought in over 2 lakhs to me. A spontaneous visit to their office with my then 6-year-old son led to an unexpected opportunity. They were launching an English News Channel and needed a female anchor. Though hesitant, I agreed to give it a try. That same day, I filmed my first video and went on to shoot over 30 videos on various national and international issues, earning some extra income along the way. What started as a simple inquiry evolved into a fulfilling journey, where passion met opportunity, and probability worked its magic!

Reflected in the same way, psychologist *Martin Seligman*—suggests that even in the face of adversity, individuals often find a source of strength when they are least expecting it. It's the unpredictability of life that can sometimes work in our favour, just as it did for you when you least anticipated it. By taking chances, even with minimal hope, you embraced the possibility of change, which is often the starting point for growth and transformation.

Viktor Frankl, a psychiatrist and Holocaust survivor, who wrote about finding meaning in suffering and the ability to choose one's attitude in any circumstance spoke about the same. Insisting that even when circumstances seem overwhelmingly bleak, taking one step forward can lead to surprising outcomes. And when you allow yourself to believe in possibilities, you allow yourself to thrive, even when you are unsure of the outcome.

The power of trying has been my foundation for survival, sustenance, and growth. Starting from the lowest rung of the ladder, I've now made it to the middle. Somewhere in the transit of life's journey, I've become an educator, a writer, an anchor, a communicator, and earned my doctorate—each one a feather in my cap. I'm deeply grateful for all the support that allowed me to try and craft my space.

Life often rewards those who keep pushing, even when the odds are stacked against them, and this journey is perhaps a beautiful example of this.

CHAPTER 2
FEAR, INSECURITIES, AND ADVANTAGE

Chapter 2
Fear, Insecurities, and Advantage

The world around us perceives us in one way or another. Prominently, we are appraised, by the way we portray ourselves to the world. Well, if we ever invite people into our insecurities, fears, and deepest thoughts, then their entire perception will change in no time. People see me as a strong, confident, and independent woman who has figured out everything. Well, I must confess that-

"I don't feel adequate, confident, and strong all the time"

"I do carry insecurities, concerns, and fears"

"I do lose in events, exams, and situations"

"I don't have solutions to all the problems"

"I have not figured out everything"

My fears about many things sneak into me, now and then. After years of an adventurous and turbulent life, I can now reflect on how fear became one of my strongest motivators. From the sheer fear of survival to the constant dread of sustaining, fear took on various shapes and knocked on my door repeatedly. Even so, there were days when two or three significant fears ran parallel, each as heavy and overwhelming as the other, coupled with the routine anxieties of daily life. I was navigating a sea of uncertainty, battling waves that threatened to drown me at every step.

Out of them, I'll narrate one here. It is about the fear of losing my mother during her heart surgery. I remember that chilling night in January 2022, when she complained of heaviness in her chest. When, despite basic home-based treatments, she couldn't feel better, I, along with my father rushed her to the hospital. There we learned that it was a silent attack and her arteries were almost one hundred percent blocked! Shedding tears silently, I was pleading before God to save her at any cost. She is a piece of heart and soul, my all-weather friend. I remember how I barely managed to keep standing on my feet after listening to this. I simply said, "Do, whatever you can do, Dr" The doctor went on hinting that usually, survival could be difficult in many of such cases.

Keeping my fears inside, I zipped up my winter jacket and asked the doctor to try his best. It was 3 am. I asked my father to remain seated at the waiting chair lying outside Operation Theatre and I went out to buy the necessary medicines prescribed and complete all paper-related formalities. Crossing my fingers, I found myself entirely soaked in that fear, agony, anxiety, helplessness, and terror badly. A bare imagination of any unforeseen moment was breaking me into two pieces and I was ready to lose whatever little I had, in return for my mother's life. Thankfully, after two hours of surgery, my mother survived that heart attack and we could bring her back home. However, those haunted scars are still on my psyche and I can still feel those chills. This was one of those defining moments that taught me to appreciate every moment and stay grateful for all that we have.

Fears have a tremendous capacity to control us. Triggered by real or perceived threats, fear is also the key to survival. A movie named 'Life of Pie (2012) portrays the survival of a young man in the disasters of an unknown sea along with a tiger in his life-saving boat. In the movie, the boy named 'Pi' is very well aware of his biggest fears- those were his biggest motivations and also led to his survival. The highs and lows of Pi's adventurous odyssey strongly resemble those of us who try to give faith a chance despite our lives full of fears, anxieties, and uncertainties. Another reality-based movie 'Cast Away' (2000) explores human life under extreme hopelessness, isolation, and physical, mental, and emotional obstacles. It portrays how a human character is formed after overcoming situations that could be one of the worst nightmares of any human on earth.

Insecurities Drive Fear

"Have you ever felt like no matter how much you've studied or accomplished, there's still a part of you that holds back? Even with great qualifications and experience, people sometimes doubt themselves. It's that quiet, nagging belief that others know more, have done more, or bring more to the table. This thought can stop them from stepping into their full brilliance, keeping their true potential hidden away. But what if that belief isn't true?"

Those securities vary from age to age. To children, insecurities may orbit around their school-work, bullying, comparing, ignorance, family conflicts, and other behavioural things. To adults, the impossible pressures of the economic world, unattainable cost of living, shackled debts, social pressures, and traumatic experiences, can cause insecurities, anxieties, and after that, fear. Digging deeper, behind any fear there is worry about looking foolish, doing something wrong, and not meeting expectations.

Why so? Because our societies are about winning. We often witness that victories are celebrated, and winners are cherished. However, for the one who loses, we have kept no room deliberately. As if human life is about ON and Off like an electric switch, with seemingly no middle room. Ignorant of the fact that success and failure are binary, we want to remain achievers and therefore, we fear failing anything short of success. More so, what seems a success today, may not seem tomorrow too!

Today, as I sit back and look at my life, I can confidently say that my journey has gradually moved in an upward direction. But I'm also painfully aware that life could have gone the other way too. There were moments when the crushing weight of circumstances almost pushed me toward a dark path—the terrifying thought of jumping into a river with my toddler in my arms. Those were moments when despair whispered that escape was the only option. Yet here I am, sharing my story of holding on to even the faintest sliver of hope. Thankfully, I could survive. We survived. And, my fears remained one of my strongest motivators in life, and I must admit that in anticipation of a horrible tomorrow, I went on working.

But as life unfolded, I began to realize that fear wasn't just an adversary—it was also a teacher. It forced me to confront my limits, question my decisions, and find hidden reserves of strength I never knew I had. Fear made me think creatively, even in the direst of moments. No matter how broken I have been, I had to get up, get ready, and wear a smile on my face just like clothes and accessories.

Fear Attracts Too

Many a times, fear is certainly not a feeling to enjoy. But trust me, fear attracts us too. We seek fear—strange as it sounds, we crave it. If this were not true then why else do so many of us love watching horror movies, even though they make us jump and scream? Why do people willingly go on adventures that put their lives at risk? Why is Mount Everest scattered with the remains of those who dared to climb it? And, despite this, why every year thousands of people dream of standing at the edge of danger, braving extreme weather and low oxygen levels?

In June 2023, The Ocean Gate Titan - a vessel, designed for deep-sea exploration—was on a dive to the Titanic wreck site when it tragically imploded, killing all five aboard. The tragedy underscores the profound interplay between fear and the human pursuit of the unknown. For the adventurers aboard, fear might have been outweighed by their curiosity and passion for exploration, but the tragic outcome demonstrates how ignoring fear can sometimes lead to dire consequences.

For these individuals, it wasn't just about being rich or famous; it was about confronting the unknown, pushing their limits, and feeling the rush of something extraordinary. The depths of the ocean, the wreckage of a lost world—it's a powerful pull, almost magnetic. The Titanic represents history, tragedy, and mystery, and being able to connect with that past, even at the risk of their lives, was a chance few would ever have again.

I've felt that pull too. I dream of doing scuba diving or skydiving someday—not because I'm fearless, but because I want to know what it feels like to face the unknown and come out stronger. It's not just about the thrill; it's about proving to myself that I can take that leap, quite literally, and feel truly alive in the process.

Moving further, on finding the 'psychology behind adventure,' I wanted to know why people love encountering the peak of fear. With no 'cookie-cutter reason, it's a mix of speed, adventure, adrenaline, and fear, and people who experience it, realize that no trivial stuff really matters. When they decide to move towards something that they were scared of; they feel empowered, transformed, and find that the usual problem of life just melts away.

"Everything that you ever wanted is on the other side of the fear."

Fear does something powerful—it wakes us up. It sharpens our senses and makes us notice every single detail of life, even the ones we usually overlook. It pulls us into the present, makes us humble, and makes us fully aware of what truly matters.

It reminds us of what we're capable of when we push past our comfort zones. Maybe that's why we don't just avoid fear; sometimes, we run toward it. Not to be reckless, but to feel that rush of courage and accomplishment on the other side. It's human to want that. It's what makes life feel real.

Fear, however, is quite an inevitable, natural, and normal part of the human experiences. We don't just experience fears in extraordinary situations like 'adventures' 'life trauma' 'skydiving' or 'scuba diving' watching classy 'horrible movies' or roaming across any haunted place at 'midnight'. Rather, fear can be felt even in ordinary circumstances like —changing the city, switching jobs, or working hard to pursue a dream, etc. Irrespective of the situation, when we embrace fear, it can be harnessed as a major driving force in life.

Being fearful of future outcomes keeps us planned, focused, informed, and alert, and saves us from facing a few possible disasters. This doesn't mean that disasters don't happen, but feelings of fear can reduce their occurrence. And that too doesn't mean that you should become a coward man. But yes, between 'flight and fight,' we should identify the right option.

However, fear serves as a critical checkpoint, prompting caution in the face of uncertainty, especially in high-risk environments. Unless you are trapped and enclosed in an 'ocean gate-like submarine or caught by 'fundamentalists,' you can try to stay immune to things going wrong, stay connected with loved ones, and practice gratitude.

Fear Owned Me a Space

Four years ago, I could manage to buy us a small living space. Initially with the support of some home loan, eventually all paid lately. When people asked me what it took me to own a house, I took a deep breath, smiled, and said it cost me hundreds of sleepless nights, half-fed days, restless intervals, teary mornings, quiet evenings, lonely weekends, and many untold stories. It cost me the pain of hearing harsh words, the scars of betrayal, the weight of wounded memories, and a vacuum where love and laughter should have been.

It cost me 'a piece of life' almost at its breaking point. But amidst all the struggle, it gave me something invaluable—a chance to rebuild. This home brought back pieces of my self-esteem, moments of genuine smiles, and a renewed sense of trust and confidence. Now, it's more than a house; it's my safe heaven. It's where I can laugh freely, cry deeply, dream again, and live fully. For this, I am endlessly thankful to the universe.

Nothing would have terrified me harder than my fear of survival and sustenance. Interestingly, the most trauma-led days have now become the most inspiring stories of my life, and are driving me through seemingly impossible means. My fear pushed me to knock on the doors to possibilities and when it was merely a 0.0001% chance of winning, I tried.

"Remember those days in the hostel? Every night before going to sleep, I'd lie awake wondering how long I could keep living there with my boy. I was told he could only stay with me until the age of 12. So, I had 6-7 years in hand. After that, he wouldn't be allowed to stay. With an income of just 35K, the thought of buying a place of my own felt impossible. That fear—of not having a home, of not being able to provide for him—pushed me harder every single day.

It became my driving force to work more, to seek every opportunity, and to never stop. I can't forget my first freelance assignment paid me just ₹70. It was a freezing

December night when I got the task. My hands were either tucked under the quilt for warmth or braving the cold to type. The client kept calling and giving instructions, and I made sure to note everything. By 1 a.m., I had finished and submitted the work. That ₹70 wasn't life-changing, but it sparked something in me. Fast forward to today, I've worked on assignments worth $7000 and more. While those larger sums are rewarding, I'll always remember that first ₹70. It wasn't just money—it was hope toward being able to rebuild life.

Without that fear, a person like me, might have never been able to own a small space. And, I might not have travelled across the lengths and breadths of this beautiful country to participate and seek work or would have not been able to send my son to a reputed convent school.

Fear of Unknown

"Out of a fear of the unknown, people prefer suffering that is familiar."

The fear of the unknown is deeply psychological, rooted in our discomfort with uncertainty. Our minds, designed to predict and control, rebel against the unpredictable, whether it's repeatedly calling loved ones to make sure if they are ok, or refreshing our inbox to check the update about that interview result, or suspecting someone is invading our privacy. Our reaction to uncertainties has actually evolved our brains to constantly predict what's next and enabled our body and mind to respond accordingly.

Imagine having a human foe, who is constantly keeping an eye on every moment of you, spying on you every now and then and making things constantly miserable by each second. For instance, when I realized someone was spying on me, I felt an immediate flood of emotions like betrayal, paranoia, and vulnerability. It was as though my world had been infiltrated, leaving me exposed and powerless. However, the experience also taught me resilience—how to protect my boundaries and regain control over my personal space and emotions. Fear, in moments like these, becomes a powerful teacher, guiding us to safeguard what matters most.

Embracing the unknown forces us to step outside our comfort zones, take risks, and trust that, even if we stumble, we can still find our way. Fear of the unknown isn't just about what we might lose—it's also about what we stand to gain.

When I first realized that someone was spying on me, a deep sense of violation washed over me. It was as if my personal space, which I had always thought of as my sanctuary, had been breached. The fear triggered was a mix of anxiety and distrust—how could I ever feel safe again knowing someone was watching me? In moments like these, my instinct was to protect myself. I withdrew, stayed alert, and began questioning everything around me. It's a challenging feeling, but one that teaches you the importance of safeguarding your privacy and emotional well-being.

Fear of Getting Replaced

An Indian Hindi language drama movie - 'Fashion' (2008) hit me hard for a reason. In one scene of that movie, the current model of a fashion company was immediately replaced by another model without any sufficient reason. And, eventually, the new model would have to experience the same soon after. Here, you would say- what is a big deal in this? In modern times, it is obvious that people get replaced - faster than before. Agreed. But to take this matter forward, would you like to recall any of the moments when you experienced a replacement? Any time by your boyfriend or girlfriend? Or your boss? Or any business partner? Or your favourite co-worker who no longer sees a favourite person in you? Or anyone else for that matter?

You take your time for at least 5 to 10 minutes and go back to those flashbacks and try to feel, the way you felt in those days. You would say, "I don't want to recall those bad and painful memories". Well, here is my point, the memories have pain, despair, and helplessness. You must have felt shattered, broken into pieces, and sometimes, that mental pain would have made you physically unwell too for a shorter or longer period. And, no incident of replacement can be more painful than that of the first incident of replacement. To be true, I don't have any key to fixing this problem.

Simply, I can only help you see through the lens of some ideas that I evolved after thinking over and over about that scene of that movie. I used to wonder a lot, about what a person does or keeps doing so that no one gets bored of him or no one tries to replace him with anyone, anytime. Well, I can begin by telling you that love yourself first.

The prerequisite of loving yourself starts with knowing yourself and giving space and time to yourself. Yeah, this process of self-exploration is so beautiful that eventually, you would not look towards people to approve or disapprove of you. In other words, if you are carrying a fear of getting replaced, and constantly working to improve yourself in the eyes of people to maintain your position, in fact, here you have already lost the game. The stance indicates that if you lose your position in other people's lives, you will also lose your position in your own life. It means you are not gonna like yourself for the reasons that, no one likes you. Or you hate yourself for being called boring and regular. This means, you are giving so much damn to the views of others on you, that your rating by them is directly related to your rating for yourself. And, they enjoy that position of keeping your control in your hand.

What truly troubles us are the after-effects of being replaced: the fear of irrelevance, the loss of identity, and the uncertainty of what comes next. But here's the thing: every ending opens a door to a new beginning. Rather than clinging to a fleeting moment, we can focus on what we leave behind—our impact, our lessons, and our growth. Because in the end, it's not about how long you stayed on the stage, but what you did while you were there.

Why this happens? People have a general tendency to get used to - in relationships, on a job, at any place, or in situations. Psychologists say that it's simply an emotion that arises due to the comfort zone of a person. However, this doesn't mean that the other person has flaws or is no longer a suitable person. Meanwhile, we as humans are not meant to pump our adrenaline and stay in

a constantly excited state. That would be a lot for a nervous system to handle.

Usually, people with easy lives feel bored in their unfulfilled desire to get drama, and conflicts to feel alive. However, it is difficult to team with people who are too wired around their narrow selfish needs and keep moving around getting or not getting entertained. Coz life is not about entertainment or excitement every time. More than a fourth of a normal person's life is about ordinary days and commoner feelings. Better is to stay aware and don't get too pushed to stay on stage every time. Allow calmness, and peaceful co-existence to yourself.

"Getting bored pertains only to the stupid people on this planet of wonder! For clever, even the simplest thing like –a sunset or sunrise- can be a great source of entertainment"

Love and Fear Paradox

On one lazy morning when I woke up to the beautiful sunrise in the best of my days, I was pretty happy and contended. Outside the window, I saw a bunch of flowers bathed in sunlight, blossomed to their full and swirling along the mild winds of winter. But as I became conscious of the feeling of love, sensation and warmth, I also found myself getting deeply saddened by its impending loss. I began to imagine the shifting of sunlight, the fragility of flower petals, their short-life and hence, loss. Beauty. Love. Fear. Loss. Hope. All occurred to me for being so real, so much in contrast and I tried to hold on to the moments by taking a picture of this in my phone. Something like producing a cheap version of nature's masterpiece.

Now, I could sense a mix of emotions inside me – of love, gratitude, fear and grief. Does that mean love has its knots tied to grief? Perhaps yes. Otherwise, what would be the capacity of any person or any object to make us feel bad or sad? Or does that mean that the eventuality of loss makes love more precious? In fact, love is a beautiful experience to be treasured for being so fragile, and so living.

The anticipation of losing someone we love, chocks us from inside. At times, we see emotional pain turning into physical pain, heartache and we try opting 'denial avoidance' cycle, until we fully encounter this. We all have such pictures or photographs that we tend to look back to again and again to cherish the beautiful time and shedding our share of tears.

We recall how badly we wanted to hold on to those moments, or make every possible effort to avoid undesirable moments and stay optimist at all cost. Unfortunately, all that had made the love more of a possession, a moment where we wanted to exercise control and it works against the living law of nature. Inevitably, the love dies.

And, then began another episode of fear and disconnection. For next time, we guard ourselves from appreciating the same beauty again, falling into the trap of love, and hence, the fear of losing. A few of us keep our lives small, controlled and limited while subconsciously knowing that we are actually protecting ourselves from getting harmed by the pain of loss and separation. Inside, they may feel stiff, hollow, empty and even dead but they may constantly strike down the idea of being in love. For them, love is fragile and hence, painful.

Heartbreaks from a partner are hard. Yet they exist. Not just to a few of us, but to most of us. For one or the other reason, if you experienced separation from your partner, it's because something else was more important to you or them than the relationship. It can be the ability to power over others, or seeking validation through intimacy or raising the adrenaline level high every now and then.

Whatever it is, it simply reflects that the values of one partner are not aligned with the other. Truly living and fully experiencing the love and its beauty seems like living two lives altogether- a powerful feeling of life into you and at the same time, putting yourself at the risk of painful fear of loss.

If randomly caught in a situation, the one who walks out from a relationship would probably say "I don't know what leads me into that. I was stressed, or maybe drunk and it was a situation that…." Allowing a black hole to consume their self-respect, they would reiterate, "It was completely an accident, it will never happen again" to keep holding on to a relationship. Meanwhile, if they peel off their self-awareness onion and say, "You know what, I was not getting what I was seeking out of our relationship.

Or maybe I care about myself more than our relationship. Or I don't have much respect for the relationship and hence, I would go on to do whatever, whenever and wherever I want". In those traps, all you can do is to shift your focus towards 'self-care, self-love' and allow yourself to forgive and forget. Though it may not quickly happen, eventually it will let you feel free, better and improved.

The essential truth is that love, while fragile, is not futile. It allows us to feel the heights of joy and depths of sorrow, helping us grow in ways we never imagined. The pain of loss is not a failure of love but an affirmation of its high impact. If we didn't love, we wouldn't feel the loss too. And in that paradox lies the beauty of life itself – to love despite the risks, to hope despite the fears, and to embrace the fleeting moments of happiness without trying to control them. It's in surrendering to this impermanence that we find true peace.

Love is not about permanence or possession but presence. We fear losing what we value the most. But fear doesn't have to define our love. Instead, it can teach us to appreciate the fleeting beauty of connection. To truly live and love is to make peace with fear, to recognize it as part of the experience rather than something to avoid.

Fear reminds us of the fragility of what we hold dear, urging us to be present, to give freely, and to embrace the moment. Like the sunlight that dances on flower petals, love is transient, yet it leaves a lasting warmth in our souls. The key is not to resist the fear of loss but to live despite it – to allow ourselves to feel deeply, knowing that even in its impermanence, love enriches us. As I gazed at the flowers and put my phone down, I realized that fear isn't a reason to retreat from love; it's a reminder of how precious it truly is.

CHAPTER 3
SOLITUDE IS NOT THAT BAD

Chapter 3
Solitude is not that bad

I will begin with the Japanese film 'Perfect Days'- a story of Hirayama, a humble toilet cleaner in the bustling city of Tokyo. The movie portrays his profound connection with nature, soulful appreciation for music, and unwavering love for books, infusing his life with a unique sense of fulfilment. Through its deliberative minimalism, the story beautifully narrates his everyday life, subtle gestures, the rhythms of daily routine, and observational power. At its core, the film beautifully portrays how solitude can yield unexpected treasures of joy, inner peace, and resilience and enduring beauty of simplicity and solitary moments, in the most unassuming lives.

Very moving, I must say that solitude reveals a lot of things. Many times, a volume of meaningless distractions consumes us, constantly divides our focus, and saps our precious time. To the extent that we are unable to appreciate our breath taking briefs and inexplicable existence in this universe. I appreciate solitude. Rather, I must say I have become quite addicted to it over a period and don't want to lose it. It has its attraction. Yeah, contrary to the popular belief that solitude is a suffering, a painful experience, and an unassuming wish, I have found a golden facet of it.

It makes me fully conscious of my state of being alive, allows me to feel the dichotomy of joys and sufferings, and discover the way pain contrasts to bring beauty to life.

A research study states singular life in a crowded world appears scary to many. People try to avoid it, overcome it, and to be true, they are fearful about it. Even so, a lot of people from all generations keep going on with their 'not-so-good' or 'unhealthy' or 'toxic' partner, because they are so much afraid of being alone. Once, one of my students approached me through a messaging app. He wanted to talk about his female friend, whom he met two weeks ago and then, had found that they both carry different ideologies and therefore, now can't be together for longer. On face, it appeared so easy to walk out from a newly found relationship, in a case when both have realized that they are not made for each other.

Alright! I asked what his problem was next. Well, his problem was not about the difference in the opinion or approach among them but was about something else. It was about the vacuum or the loneliness that the person will have after parting ways. Sensing that trauma of loneliness, he would continue to take the pain of carrying forward with an un-futuristic relation. Yeah, loneliness gives a vacuum, and it's painful, but he had to choose the better pain. I mean, the least bad option. And, to him, he found continuing with the relationship would pain him less than dealing with a vacuum.

Psychologists name it- Auto-phobia, Monophobia, or Eremophobia - which means a feeling of intense fear of being by yourself, or spending time alone, or in solitude, etc. Studies say that around 7.4% of people in the world face this mental condition at one or the other time in their lifetimes, particularly, when they are alone, or anticipating being alone, or when they are excluded from a group, etc. Such people would go to extreme lengths to avoid being isolated.

American Psychologist Association says that people can experience such traumas at any juncture in life. It disrupts your normal daily life, your decision-making, and also, your overall personality. Undoubtedly, it's normal to be around people. However, being alone is also inevitable in life, at one point or another; therefore, we should have the ability to sail through those situations as well. To be honest, it's not that easy or that difficult. We also wish to have solitude, want to be around people or be a part of gossip while sitting on the drawing room couch. Yeah, we do enjoy almost every component in our own way or pace.

As a writer, I understand the relevance of solitude. It's been quite a few times when I randomly travelled to experience a beach walk or to watch a sunset through the hills. That cosy and dusky evening that was getting darker and darker with each passing moment, that roar of the majestic sea, those waves touching my bare feet, and that wet sand beneath my foot were cooling down my mind from all that chaos. It reminded me that the essence and worth of this universe are beyond our imaginations.

Truly, those evenings allowed me to zoom out of worries, apprehensions, and fears. At times, doing things your way with minimum distractions, opinions, or influences is good for mental well-being and increases your feeling of peace and acceptability within. It gets you better concentration, productivity, and creativity and makes you more empathetic. However, our desire for alone time is influenced by our personalities. Extroverts dislike it and introverts prefer it. Of course, just because you are an introvert, doesn't mean that you want to be alone each time. Social engagements make sense in our lives, and we need them too. As long as you can balance it, you can experience a brighter side of it.

If You Don't Know Solitude, You Don't Know Freedom

Grigori Perelman, a Russian-born Jewish mathematician, is celebrated for solving the Poincaré Conjecture, one of the seven Clay Millennium Prize Problems, a ground breaking achievement that earned him both a Fields Medal and the $1,000,000 Millennium Prize.

However, Perelman declined both honours, citing the collaborative nature of mathematical progress and deeming it "unfair" to other mathematicians who made significant contributions. Known for his deep aversion to the spotlight, he has led a reclusive life in St. Petersburg, Russia, avoiding public appearances and interviews since 2006.

His urge for solitude was poignantly expressed during a rare encounter with a journalist seeking an interview. He famously replied, "You are disturbing me. I am picking mushrooms," underscoring his preference for a quiet, contemplative life immersed in nature over the distractions of fame and recognition.

Dr. A.P.J. Abdul Kalam, one of India's most revered figures, is remembered not only for his immense contributions to science and technology but also for his humility and unwavering dedication. Known as the "Missile Man of India" for his pioneering work in the country's space and missile programs, Kalam embodied a rare combination of brilliance and simplicity. Despite his ground breaking achievements, he consistently shunned the spotlight, avoiding lavish ceremonies and public recognition.

Once, during his tenure as the President of India, he was invited to a lavish dinner hosted by a foreign dignitary. The event was filled with diplomats, high-ranking officials, and prominent figures, all dressed in formal attire and engaged in high-level discussions.

Despite being the president, Dr. Kalam surprised everyone when he declined the extravagant meal and opted for a simple vegetarian dish, chose to sit in a corner of the room, away from the formalities, and ate his meal quietly, enjoying the simplicity of it. In his lifetime, he focused on his true callings of solitude and simplicity, staying grounded and true to his purpose.

Perelman's and Dr Kalam's story powerfully reminds us that true genius often flourishes in silence, and the pursuit of knowledge can transcend worldly accolades, reflecting a life dedicated to intellectual purity and inner peace.

Joy of Solo Escapes

Have you ever tried watching a movie all alone? Yeah, it may seem odd and surreal to experience, but I am sure you will not feel the same after doing that the first time. We must admit that there are a lot of examples of people watching movies alone, or finding shows with minimal audience possible to even booking the entire theatre to consume the movie entirely.

Here, I am not against a group movie experience. I can't deny that having fun in a group is a great thing. However, I simply want to say that the experience of solitude is also not that bad.

I am sure your sole experience of 'watching a movie' or 'sipping a coffee' or 'reading a book' would have been much richer in terms of focus, freedom, and comfort with minimal distractions. Yeah, I haven't done a ton of research to arrive at a single way to enjoy solitude, but anecdotally I found such experiences are not that bad.

Let me confess that I have watched a number of movies all alone and therefore I can differentiate whenever I have been watching it with someone else. I found myself watching it through their eyes, emotions, and sentiments in addition to my own. And, it is enough to ruin your wholesome movie experience when the movie really needs to be filtered through you and your brain only.

Taking you through another experience of 'sipping coffee all alone' at a coffee shop, I visit coffee shops quite often and see a lot of people coming and going, staring at each other, flaunting their dresses, or maybe handling kids. Quite often, in one particular shop, I would cherish the presence of a middle-aged man who would come there with his book and choose any corner table to sit at.

He will barely talk, except when ordering something. Among a variety of visitors, blending cappuccinos then putting whipping cream on it with some names, all I could think was "This man must be a writer." Well, being a writer by myself, it's not unusual for me to understand how much I enjoy doing the same.

Just like that man, I would find a cosy corner with a laptop and start writing about anything that I could think of. I prefer staying focused when it comes to doing my tasks; also, I tried to do my tasks together to see what all the fuss about working together is.

To be clear, I am neither comparing nor criticizing teamwork nor a group activity. At the same time, I am asserting that we should not create an uproar around group obsession, and must reduce dependency. Solitude allows us to communicate within ourselves. And, just like any other thing, our 'self' also needs to be taken care of, and also, needs to be heard of.

Together and Alone - Solitude in Groups

Have you ever felt like an outsider despite being a part of a group or surrounded by people? Something like that you are on the edge of every friend group and have no 'go-to' person. Psychologists call it 'thwarted belongingness' – a persistent state of not fitting in any of the social circles. Such a state of feeling unseen, unheard and uncared for can impact our well-being in various ways.

And, when we repeatedly feel that we don't belong to, we internalise that we are unimportant, unlovable and burdened, and therefore, intensify existing insecurities. Moreover, no matter how subtle, the feeling of rejection can add to this cycle

Now, think of answering this question. Why do we look for a group or any association? One, it gives us acceptance and identity. Two, it meets our socialization needs. Three, we gain information and do social comparisons as a part of the group. Additionally, it serves our need to seek approval and validation of our beliefs, thoughts, actions, and decisions.

Despite claiming and rejoicing in the feeling of being independent, we enjoy approvals. To the extent that we want people to constantly remind us that – we are great, we have been great, and we continue to stay great, no matter what! It actually empowers. That means, we are almost never independent enough to validate our opinion; rather, we want other people to say it. Yeah, we all do that.

Imagine when that person said something bad about you, you felt sad and angry. Right? And, in the other time that one appreciation had made your day. Isn't it? Knowingly or unknowingly, our remote control stays in the hands of other people. And, let me tell you that this approach is likely to disappoint you, most of the time. Don't get me wrong, I too love to go out with friends, have conversations, share thoughts and even laugh loudly with them at funny Instagram reels. Agreeing with the fundamental desire for social recognition, I must say that it works in reverse order too, when the group excludes or outcasts you, or doesn't let you feel emotionally safe for being different. Moreover, if everyone in the group didn't feel equal and found the group controlled by one or two individuals, it would turn into a giant mess experience towards the end. And, you will feel alone in this togetherness!

Now, imagine putting 5 to 10 mortally different people together in a room and compelling them to be together for a day. What would you expect? Emotions will spill over, and these people will jostle from topic to time.

Practically, even the most kind-hearted person in the group would either try to become the centre of attention or slink away into the silence halfway with a nod or say 'sorry' with a quick shuffle out of the room. Perhaps, they were there till they got balm on their psychological wounds – not to become the audience for someone else. Undeniably, your emotions are not attended well and your need for connection remained unfulfilled.

We all have to combat situations like career instability, problematic friendships, difficulty in expression, extreme moods, multiple phobias, cultural dissimilarities, etc, at one or the other time. In such a scenario, we barely speak about our feelings, though they still flow out through our interaction. If I say to any of my friends, I'm sorry, I don't want to talk, I want to go home," and he doesn't ask why, or not wondering if I'm ok or not, perhaps our wavelengths are not matching.

And, in such high-pressure environments, people quickly judge your stories and compare them with theirs. Even so, they still find their problems bigger than your problems. They justify your pain with one or the other fact, though they would never justify their own.

Here, one can say that- this also doesn't mean that we should live lonely. Yes, absolutely, not. Sometimes, it's surprising what (or who) may be waiting right around the corner for deep connections, friendships and genuine belongings alongside practising solitude. Find them!

Abysses of Solitude

Emily Dickinson, one of America's greatest poets, embraced solitude in a way that allowed her to cultivate a deeply introspective and creative life. While she spent much of her time in her home in Amherst, Massachusetts, her reclusive nature was not out of despair but rather a deliberate choice that enabled her to focus intensely on her poetry.

By maintaining a small circle of close relationships, Dickinson found the space to explore profound themes of life, nature, and the human experience, all while developing a unique voice that would eventually resonate with generations of readers. Though her works were largely unpublished during her lifetime, her solitary existence gave birth to some of the most insightful and impactful poetry in American literature, where the themes of isolation were often depicted as moments of personal reflection and intellectual depth.

Whenever you find solitude, allow it to seep in to feel your existence as a larger part of this universe and derive the profundity through it.

My solitude has magically empowered me with a lot of space, time, and energy. It created an ecosystem for thoughts to pop up, words to surface, and ideas to grow. Quite often, I have swum through those deep depths of my subconscious mind and found a treasure of possibilities, and passions. Plenty of those possibilities have worked. Ironically, no 'thought lab' would have done the same.

Out of many things that I like doing in solitude, a few are - looking at the birds flying, watching squirrels collecting food, watching out of my office window, viewing the sky, or if possible, ocean waves, listening to the roars of nature, decorating my physical space and of course, writing. I like the shades of nature for being gentle to moderate and extreme. Its gentleness reminds me of those sweet and sour tastes that I witness in a single life. Moreover, its roar empowers me to conquer my fears and worries, and, assert that nothing is going to last forever. To be true, it aligns my inner and outer self with the wisdom of the world. At times fascinating, and at times authoritative, those mystics of this 'mother nature' teach philosophical lessons to connect deeply with solitude.

If this had not been so true, why would saints' value and practice solitude? Why would there have been so much talk around practising meditation? Significantly, we must acknowledge that all cultures and religions endorse solitariness for a path to self-discovery. In case you are afraid of being alone, you are actually afraid to accept your existence. It could be your naked and honest existence in the deceptive world around you, but you don't allow yourself to know it because that can cause discomfort. And, when you don't nurture this basic understanding of your existence, you won't be able to make conscious choices, find meaning and purpose in life, build authentic relationships, and do things that matter.

But one doesn't need to be in 'solitude' forever, however, for a period and times, yes, one should. Meditation and solitude have been central themes in the lives of many revered figures across religions. Lord Shiva, often meditating on Mount Kailash, symbolizes transcendence in Hinduism. Gautama Buddha achieved enlightenment under the Bodhi tree after deep solitary reflection. Prophet Muhammad received revelations in the solitude of the Cave of Hira. Jesus Christ fasted and meditated for 40 days in the wilderness, while Mahavira's ascetic meditation led to omniscience in Jainism. Tested across times, seclusion has served as a powerful medium for spiritual growth, wisdom, and profound revelations across traditions.

Self-Space Has Boundaries

Moving next to group therapies, let's talk about personal space- a gateway to solitude in our everyday lives.

Personal space isn't just about the physical space that we keep from others—it's also about the emotional boundaries we create to feel safe and comfortable. Think of it as a "buffer zone" that protects our sense of self and allows us to navigate relationships with confidence.

This buffer isn't one-size-fits-all. Rather, it's shaped by who we are—our background, culture, and the social situations we find ourselves in. For some, boundaries come naturally and are healthy, creating space for mutual respect and trust. For others, boundaries might be too rigid or too loose, leaving them feeling disconnected or scattered.

Many of us often struggle with boundaries when we either let people overstep them or build walls that keep everyone out.

Here are some routine examples of poor boundaries-

- *"You can't talk to her. You know how bad I feel when you speak to her. It's better if you stay away."* This shifts the speaker's emotional responsibility onto someone else, demanding control over their actions to soothe personal insecurities.

- *"Listen, you're new to this organization, and as your boss, I must tell you who to speak to and who not to."* Here, authority is used to impose unnecessary control, crossing professional boundaries.

- *"I love to keep an eye on every single detail of your life. After all, this is how I can take care of you."* While this might sound caring on the surface, it's a classic example of overstepping boundaries under the guise of concern.

- *"That man doesn't belong to our region. If you want to stay part of this group, don't meet up with him."* This reflects a group dynamic that enforces boundaries based on exclusion and control, limiting individual autonomy.

- *"I wish I could come along, but I'm sure my best friend would dislike it."* Here, the speaker avoids responsibility for their own choices by deflecting it onto someone else.

- *"Allow me to check your phone every now and then. I'll decide what's good and bad for you."* This invades personal privacy and dismisses the other person's autonomy.

- *"Keep sharing your location details with me every day."* While this might seem like a safety measure, it often masks mistrust or a need for control.

These plenty of examples state that people with poor boundaries either try to overstep others' self-space or allow their own space to be overrun.

On the flip side, analyse these tones with healthy and workable boundaries-

- *"I hear what you're saying, but I need some time to process my thoughts before responding. Let's revisit this tomorrow."* This shows emotional maturity and self-awareness, allowing space to respond thoughtfully instead of reacting impulsively.

- *"I'm not comfortable with hugs, but I'd love to shake hands or give you a friendly wave!"* A clear yet kind way to assert physical boundaries while maintaining warmth.

- *"I don't check emails after 6 p.m. to spend time with my family. I'll get back to you first thing in the morning."* A polite but firm boundary that protects personal time without being dismissive.

- *"I understand you have a different perspective, but this is the decision that feels right for me."* A confident statement that honours personal agency while respecting differing opinions.

- *"I appreciate your input, but I prefer to form my own opinions about people. Thanks for understanding."* Politely pushing back against group pressure without escalating tension.

- *"I know you're asking because you care, but I'd rather keep that part of my life private."* A respectful way to decline answering to intrusive questions.

Boundaries in Familial Setups are most difficult to maintain particularly in intimate relationships when there is almost a predictable oscillation between two people. Something like two weeks of bliss, one week of hell, one month of bliss, another week of hell, breakups, romantic reunions and so on. This push-and-pull often reflects an underlying difficulty in respecting and maintaining personal boundaries within the relationship. Without clear boundaries, the relationship becomes a rollercoaster of highs and lows, fuelled by emotional dependency rather than mutual respect. As mentioned by Mark Manson, people with poor boundaries come with two approaches- Victim and Saver approach- Poor 'self-space' boundaries people seem like either 'savers'- who take too much responsibility for the actions and emotions of others, or 'victims' – who want others to take too much responsibility for their emotions and actions. Their pathology perfectly pairs with each other and they follow the model of a 'happy' relationship based on a perpetual need to play either role.

The victim often externalizes their struggles, and keeps blaming others for their actions and decisions. They would constantly paint themselves as 'someone to be rescued.' For them, it's their way of seeking love, validation, and support—by eliciting pity or care. Meanwhile, the saver thrives on solving problems, believing their worth comes from fixing others' lives. Yet, this dynamic rarely meets either person's deeper emotional needs. The victim creates endless problems to sustain the relationship, and the saver exhausts themselves trying to fix them. Ultimately, neither feels truly supported, as their roles prevent genuine connection or mutual growth.

When both see themselves as victims, they remain trapped in blame and helplessness, preventing growth. If both are savers, they exhaust themselves trying to fix each other, neglecting their own needs, leading to burnout. The healthiest relationships are built on mutual responsibility, open communication, and respect, where both partners support each other while maintaining their individuality and boundaries.

Parenthood and Boundaries

"In the sweetness of parenthood, where love knows no bounds, the strength to set healthy boundaries paves the way for growth and wisdom."

I learned the importance of boundaries from both- my father and mother. They taught me how to respect myself and others by setting clear limits and maintaining healthy relationships. This lesson has greatly influenced the way I raise my son, ensuring that he understands the value of personal space, mutual respect, and emotional boundaries.

Passing on this legacy, I raised my son with a deep sense of equality, treating him more as a peer than just a child. We shared countless moments—crying, playing, and sleeping side by side—caring for each other in a profoundly mutual way. Over time, I watched the dynamics between us evolve, as my mischievous toddler transformed into a remarkably responsible young man by the age of 12!

"The truth is, every son raised by a single mom is pretty much born - married."

I made sure to teach him about boundaries. It wasn't just about the usual rules; it was about understanding what to share, what not to share, where it's appropriate to speak up, and where it's best to listen. I wanted him to know that some things are meant to be kept private, and that not every situation requires a response. It's not just about being polite, but also about being aware of the right time and place for everything. These lessons helped him understand the balance between expressing himself and respecting the world around him.

Also, whenever needed, I defended his boundaries, took his side, became his voice, and protected him from anyone who tried to overstep. I ensured that no one walked over our space, our time, our energy, or our relationship. When people overstep, whether by offering unsolicited advice, prying into your life, or demanding more than you can give, it can feel overwhelming and intrusive. Your time, energy, and space are already stretched thin as you juggle responsibilities, and it's essential to protect them.

Setting clear boundaries isn't selfish; it's a way to ensure you can show up as your best self for both yourself and others. It's okay to say "no" or express discomfort when someone crosses a line. For example, if someone tries to impose their opinions on your parenting choices or gets too involved in your personal matters, you can gently but firmly respond with something like, "I appreciate your concern, but I'm comfortable handling this in my own way." Protecting your space doesn't mean pushing others away—it's about creating an environment where you feel safe, respected, and supported. By standing firm in your boundaries, you teach others how to treat you and set an example of self-respect for your child.

Meanwhile, your child is still learning how to navigate relationships and interactions, and they rely on you to model healthy boundaries. If someone oversteps with your child—whether by questioning your parenting in front of them, trying to discipline them without your consent, or disregarding their comfort—you have every right to step in. For instance, you might say, "I appreciate your intentions, but I'd prefer if you discuss any concerns with me privately instead of involving my child."

By setting these boundaries, you not only safeguard your child's emotional well-being but also teach them the value of self-respect and personal autonomy. It's empowering for a child to see their parent stand up for them, and it reassures them that their feelings and space matter. In doing so, you create a foundation of trust and security, showing them how to establish and maintain their own boundaries as they grow.

Boundaries and Self-Esteem –Intertwined

Self-space and personal boundaries go hand in hand with self-esteem. Higher the self-esteem, the stronger the self-space and boundaries will be. People with strong self-esteem are more likely to set healthy boundaries because they value their own needs and respect the needs of others. They understand that saying "no" isn't selfish—it's necessary. Similarly, respecting others' boundaries reflects emotional maturity and a sense of security.

Imagine a friend who always asks deeply personal questions the moment you meet. If you're not ready to share, you might feel uncomfortable, as if they've crossed an invisible line. On the other hand, a co-worker who consistently respects your time and only asks work-related questions during office hours shows an understanding of boundaries. On the other hand, weak boundaries often stem from low self-esteem. People may be over-accommodating, seek constant validations, keep a desire to control and feel unworthy of asserting their needs. Think of someone who agrees to every request, even when they're overwhelmed, because they don't want to disappoint anyone. Or someone who avoids vulnerability altogether, afraid that opening up will make them too exposed.

Be it practising solitude, protecting personal space, or defining boundaries, the hustle and bustle of daily life often makes us lose sight of their significance. But we shall consciously carve out moments for ourselves to recharge, and reflect. These aren't about shutting people out—they're about taking care of ourselves so we can show up as our best selves for others.

Solitude gives us a chance to recharge and reconnect with who we are, while personal space allows us to breathe, and feel grounded and safe. Boundaries, then, help us protect our energy and emotions, making sure we're not overwhelmed or drained. When we embrace solitude, we recharge and find clarity. When we establish personal space, we create room for peace and growth. And when we set boundaries, we ensure that our needs are respected, and our relationships remain healthy.

Together, they allow us to create a life that's not only more balanced but also more fulfilling. We stop relying on others to define our worth or solve our problems, and instead, we take responsibility for our own lives. At the same time, we're better able to show up for the people we care about, with a clear sense of who we are and what we need. In this way, we individually and collectively can lead better lives, and can happily co-exist.

CHAPTER 4
THAT PRESSURE OF BEING HAPPY

Chapter 4
That Pressure of Being Happy

In August 2022, I was attending a workshop on Human Values and Ethics in Punjab. It was a packed schedule from 9 AM to 6 PM. Around 40 participants had to attend and maintain at least 90% of attendance at all the sessions.

We had to sit on the mats in the morning and listen to the expert speaker who would go on speaking about any 'good' topic entire day and zero down on the 'idea of being happy.' The resource person spoke about how whatever we do, whatever we plan, or whatever we get—happiness is central to all those plans. And, we all must stay forever happy and feel positive—no matter what. Absolutely fine! Undeniably, I too want to be happy. But all the time? Is that possible even? Knowing that unhappiness is bound to occur, I could not agree much with that 'all-time happy' approach. Because that seems too practical. Isn't it?

Well, a few among us raised certain questions, narrated various situations, and tried to understand how someone can be happy all the time. Particularly, when their life is pissing them off. Alright, the spokesperson was very well-equipped to answer such questions with all calmness and positivity and reiterated his favourite idea that at any cost, you have to feel happy.

To everyone, it was the last achievement on this earth. Agreed? No! I couldn't agree to that, even on the third day of his teaching.

Why? Umm, I guess because I was taking too much pressure to stay happy. And that too, being happy all the time! This very pressure of fixing all the things to fix one thing, i.e., 'happiness,' is actually making me nervous. How will I be able to do that? What if I fail? What if things don't fall in line? Now, the route to happiness was actually appearing full of 'struggles, sufferings, worries, pain and sadness,' to me.

Does that mean happiness is a fake emotion? I mean, is it a phoney notion, and we shall not chase it? No. Then, what? Well, I must say that - Don't take too much pressure of it. Don't feel extremely pushed and pulled for staying happy 'all-the-time'. You may chase it if you like chasing it, but without being ignorant of the real world. Don't forget that in the real world, disasters happen, people have trouble, situations demand, experiments fail, and yes, your shit stinks.

Constant Happiness is Deception

Kirk Schneider, a psychologist, calls happiness "potential fool's gold," reminding us that the compulsion to think positive—what we often call toxic positivity—can be just as harmful as constantly thinking negative. He believes this pressure to always stay happy can actually block us from experiencing the full richness of life. By embracing our negative emotions, we add depth to our human experience, broaden our emotional vocabulary and tap into a wider range of coping skills.

Friedrich Nietzsche- a German classical scholar and philosopher, in his work 'Beyond Good and Evil', questioned the basis of good and evil. Further, it suggests that people often overcompensate for their internal struggles by projecting an image of strength or joy. While these displays can appear as confidence or vitality, they may be a form of self-deception, where the person is trying to convince themselves of their own happiness or worth. True emotional balance, according to these philosophies, comes not from constant highs but from accepting and integrating both joy and sorrow as part of the human experience.

Buddhism further supports this by identifying suffering (Dukkha) as an intrinsic part of life, essential for achieving liberation and peace. Stoicism echoes this, advocating acceptance of life's adversities as aligning with nature's order. Even Sufism, through the divine balance of Jalal (hardship) and Jamal (ease), underscores that life's completeness arises from embracing both extremes. Together, these philosophies affirm that denying unhappiness disrupts the equilibrium essential for a meaningful and harmonious existence leading to imbalance and suffering.

Heraclitus's Greek philosophy teaches that opposites create harmony, where the tension between joy and sorrow fuels the essence of life. Hinduism's concept of Samsara reflects the cyclical nature of existence, where pleasure and pain, success and failure, are necessary for growth and transformation. Similarly, Taoism's Yin and Yang demonstrate that darkness and light, sorrow and joy, are interdependent, each giving meaning to the other.

Imagine someone around you, who is always pretending to be upbeat and happy, even when facing challenges or feeling stressed; everyone around would perceive the person eventually inauthentic or anxious. Also, it prevents the person from acknowledging and addressing the real issues affecting their well-being. People who are always showing high moods might be trying to convince themselves or others that they're happy, even if deep down they're not. It's like putting on a mask to hide feelings of emptiness or insecurity.

Denying unhappiness is akin to rejecting the natural cycle of life, as emphasized by various philosophies that uphold the balance of opposites. Constant happiness, especially if it's forced or unrealistic, can create pressure to suppress negative feelings like sadness, frustration, or fear. These emotions, though unpleasant, are important for personal growth, and self-awareness and help us navigate life more meaningfully.

Happiness Vs Pleasure

It's a tragic irony that we're often so bad at knowing what will truly make us happy. We chase after things—

success, wealth, approval—thinking they'll bring us joy, only to find that they don't.

Pleasure is to the sensory organ what happiness is to the soul—temporary versus lasting. Aristotle explained this beautifully in his idea of Eudaimonia, which is about true happiness. He pointed out that while sensory pleasures, (hedone) might make us feel good for a moment, they don't last. Real happiness, according to him, comes from living a meaningful and virtuous life, where we grow, fulfil our potential, and nurture our souls. It's not about indulging in physical comforts but about flourishing as a person and finding purpose in life.

Pleasure is like a quick burst of joy, something that brightens the moment but fades away soon after. It's often tied to sensory experiences—like savouring a favourite meal, getting a compliment, or buying something bigger. While these moments feel good, they tend to be short-lived. It's like getting a temporary high that leaves you craving more, but not necessarily brings lasting fulfillment.

I think that also sums up how we — dating app generations—approach relationships. We want intimacy but neither commitment, nor strings. We want the joy of love without the effort, the promises, or the sacrifices that come with it. And we got it. But the results weren't what we hoped for. Instead of feeling fulfilled, we're left emptier than before. The closeness feels shallow, and the connections leave us still longing. So, where is true joy? Perhaps, in the bonds built on faithfulness and rooted in commitment—the kind of love that reflects something greater than ourselves. We often find ourselves seeking new pleasures, only to realize that they don't provide lasting satisfaction. Pleasures can be like drug addiction, random sex, and excessive travelling—things that feel really good at the moment but often leave you wanting more, without any lasting satisfaction.

Ask a drug user, and they might tell you how the high feels amazing at first, but over time, it takes more to get the same feeling, leaving them trapped in a cycle of emptiness and addiction. Ask a frequent traveller, and they might share how the thrill of new places fades once the excitement wears off, leaving them feeling disconnected or even more restless than before. Ask a shopaholic, and they may admit how the rush of buying something new is short-lived, only for them to find themselves chasing the next purchase, still feeling unfulfilled. Ask a food lover, and they might say that while indulging in their favourite meals brings momentary joy, it doesn't last, and they're left craving for—something that can't be satisfied by food alone. More so, gambling or over-consumption of alcohol or chasing social media can be similar quick escapes, offering a rush of emotions, but gambling can be a quick escape, offering the rush of emotions, or a temporary boost but it often leaves us emotionally empty, disconnected and anxious. It hardly aligns with long-term happiness.

"Happiness is not pleasure - it is victory."

Happiness isn't about chasing quick thrills; it's more like a steady light that comes from deeper, lasting sources. It comes from things like meaningful relationships, having a purpose, growing as a person, and living according to your values. For example, spending quality time with loved ones—like having a good chat with a friend or playing with your kids—gives you a sense of warmth that stays with you.

Achieving personal goals, like running a marathon or learning something new, feels much more rewarding than any quick win. Happiness also comes from doing kind things—helping a neighbour, volunteering, or being there for a friend. These actions give you a sense of fulfilment. Personal growth—like reading a book that changes how you think or learning a new skill—can also bring happiness, as it helps you feel more connected to yourself and the world. True happiness comes from within and stays steady, even during tough times. It's not about being happy all the time, but finding joy in life's journey, learning from struggles, and being kind to yourself when things don't go as planned. The beauty of happiness might be in its complexity, where the messy moments create the most fulfilment.

Chasing Happiness is a Trap

Chasing is exhausting. Not just physically, but also mentally, emotionally, and spiritually. What if life is not about being chased? What if it's meant to be attracted? I mean, instead of running after something, won't it be better if we ourselves become attractive enough to receive it?

Love, success, and happiness— the more we chase them, the more they seem to slip away. Many of us, in this never-ending race to find happiness, have forgotten to enjoy what's right in front of us.

Ever felt like this? Then, you're not alone.

Steve Jobs, the co-founder of Apple, once admitted that while building a world-changing company, his greatest happiness came from reconnecting with family and relationships—not from the relentless pursuit of success. It's a reminder to pause and ask, *"Am I appreciating the little things that matter most?"*

Jim Carrey, the renowned Canadian-American actor, and the comedian has once openly discussed how achieving fame and fortune didn't bring him the happiness he expected. Despite his immense success in Hollywood, he struggled with feelings of emptiness and depression. He famously said, *"I think everybody should get rich and famous and do everything they ever dreamed of so they can see that it's not the answer."* This reflects the idea that chasing external validation or material success as a substitute for inner contentment often leads to disillusionment. He later found greater fulfilment through art, spirituality, and living in the moment.

"To be happy at home is the ultimate result of all ambition."

We often treat happiness like a destination but not like a journey, believing that once we "arrive" we'll stay there forever. But life doesn't work that way. This approach has flaws. One, we will forget to enjoy the journey itself and second, that fleeting sense of happiness became obsolete the next moment. Something like, what you have achieved is not going to attract you anymore.

Also, we immediately start hunting for what's next and stuck in a cycle of always wanting more. This led to continuous frustration and missing contentment. We failed to acknowledge that real strength lay in making ourselves capable and aware enough to receive it.

So, the takeaway? Instead of chasing, attract happiness. Yeah, attraction works opposite to chasing. It simply means that you know you are worthy to receive it. Without needing external approvals or validations, you are secure, confident, and fully aware of your own magnetic charm!

Horizons of Happiness

Happiness comes with solving 'problems'

Happiness isn't a simple pursuit—it's a deeply personal, ever-changing journey. It's neither found in problems nor in solutions; rather, found in the process itself. Imagine how a brainy child feels after solving a complex mathematical problem or an adult after cracking a tough deal. Says, the joy and happiness come not from the end result, but from navigating through complexities, and exercising logical thinking, and problem-solving abilities.

That doesn't mean life won't throw difficult questions your way—challenges are inevitable. Life questions everyone, and while some questions can be tougher than others, no one can escape being questioned. It's certainly going to happen. Challenges test our abilities and resilience, pushing us to confront uncertainties and see transformations. Whether we tackle them willingly or reluctantly, we must find a way out by revising, re-routing, and re-evaluating ourselves.

Take Michael Phelps- one of the most decorated Olympians in history. After retiring, he felt lost. For years, his identity was tied to swimming, and when that chapter ended, he struggled to find purpose. His experience shows that life isn't just about achieving; it's about redefining what matters as life evolves. Phelps eventually found joy and fulfilment in mental health advocacy.

Haven't we all felt a little like this? Maybe after finishing college, changing jobs, or completing a big project? I know I'll certainly cry loudly after finishing writing this book!

We often think that reaching a goal will bring endless joy, but life doesn't always work that way. In reality, happiness is not linear or guaranteed, even when we achieve what we once thought would bring fulfilment. It's complex, unpredictable, and often shaped by the journey, not just the destination.

"Problems give us purpose and purpose give us identity"

Isn't this an interesting thought? Our problems give us purpose, and those purposes shape who we are. Think about getting fit after being out of shape for a while. At first, working out feels like a chore—your muscles are sore, and progress seems slow. But as you keep pushing through, you start to notice improvements in your strength and energy. Eventually, all that purpose-driven hard work pays off, and reaching your fitness goals brings a sense of pride and happiness. The struggle makes the success feel even sweeter.

Problems Give Us Purpose- Every challenge we face—whether in our personal lives, at work, or even in daily tasks—makes us ask, "How do I solve this?" That search for solutions gives us direction. It gives us something to work towards, something that keeps us moving forward. Without problems, there'd be no reason to grow or push ourselves beyond our comfort zones.

Purpose Gives Us Identity- How we respond to problems shows our values, strengths, and who we are. For example, someone who loves solving tough problems might see themselves as a thinker or an innovator. The purpose we find in overcoming challenges becomes a part of our identity, guiding our choices and ambitions. It's that sense of purpose that helps define who we are and gives us a clear path forward.

"The toughest problems are meant for the Nobel prizes"

The Mountain Man, or Dashrath Manjhi- a poor labour from a village in Bihar, India, single-handedly carved a path through a mountain to connect his village to the nearest town, which was 70 kilometres away. This task took him 22 years, using only a hammer and chisel, all driven by the pain of his wife's death, who couldn't receive timely medical help due to the difficult terrain. His story powerfully relates to the idea that his problem gave him a purpose in life and eventually an identity. Following it, he found his true happiness and fulfilment by making it possible, which otherwise seems impossible.

Harekala Hajabba- a humble fruit vendor from a small village in Mangalore, Karnataka won the Padma Shri in 2021. His motive? For many years, when foreign tourists asked him the price of an orange in English, he did not understand what had been said and felt embarrassed. Although Hajabba had been selling oranges for years, he didn't know the English word for it due to illiteracy. That thing sparked a realization in him about the importance of education, and he found his purpose. Driven by this, Hajabba built a primary school with his earnings of Rs 150 per day and by the year 2000, the Karnataka State Government officially recognized his initiative. Today, his school stands as a powerful symbol of selflessness and determination, proving that one person's drive to make a difference can create lasting change.

"Trailblazers don't just solve problems—they change the course of history."

More often, the harder the problem, the greater the joy when you overcome it. It's like the sense of accomplishment is directly tied to the challenge itself.

Of course, that doesn't mean that you invite problems, and solve them to feel better. No. But many times, you don't have a choice but to accept the occurrence of problems and work for them. Now, whenever they occur, don't see them as 'just worries' but try viewing them as opportunities to exhibit your ability and excellence. Yeah, it may seems like- easier said than done. But with your perception, perhaps, your modus-operands will change and things may fall better off.

More so, when you tackle something difficult, the effort and perseverance required would make the reward even sweeter. That feeling of triumph after pushing through tough situations is unmatched—it's not just about solving the problem, but about proving to yourself that you can handle them. Indifferently, these triumphs across the 'mess' will be cherished by you and your generations as 'stories of success'!

Happiness often lies in making choices for a better tomorrow. When we face challenges, we are forced to find solutions, adapt, and grow. This process helps define who we are and what we stand for. In essence, the problems we face and the purpose they create give us a framework for understanding ourselves. They make us who we are, not just by what we achieve, but by how we approach and overcome the challenges life throws our way.

Happiness is about "Travel, Sky and Stories'

'Not all those who wander are lost'

I love travelling. Travel has connected me with the world, and honestly, I found it one of my greatest sources of happiness. I love travelling so much that I couldn't possibly do justice to this book without talking about it. Luckily, I've had the chance to explore all across India — a country that's like a melting pot of civilizations and cultures. It's got everything- history, heritage, amazing food, and stunning nature. Travelling has made me a better person — more humble, more tolerant, and definitely more open-minded. It has shown me that deep down, people everywhere are so similar.

We all have our own lives, problems, and concerns, but they're often not that different from one another.

With travel, you learn that the world fantastically functions with or without the rules that we once believed as the sole truth of earth. Just like, I hail from a society where patriarchy is deeply rooted in traditions and mindsets. But when I visited places where matriarchal societies flourish, it completely changed how I see the world. It was so liberating to see women confidently leading decisions and running families and communities and it made me reflect on the unnecessary rigidity I had been accustomed to. On the flip side, I've also been to very conservative places where women didn't even have basic rights or freedoms. That stark contrast made me reflect on my own life, and I started appreciating the freedom I have to move, think, and express myself. Those experiences opened my eyes to how diverse the world is and how important it is to challenge the status quo when it comes to equality.

Honestly, travelling is like a spark for new ideas and fresh perspectives. There's no mystery in how the woods feel connected to otherworldly places, just like there's no mystery in the happiness we find in travel. Anyone who's ever walked through the woods or explored a new place knows—they're full of connections, like a constant call and response. When we travel, moments, places, and people seem to connect in unexpected ways—a smile from a stranger might remind you of a friend back home, or a local dish might bring back memories of a meal you once had with loved ones. Just as the forest ties its elements together in surprising harmony, travel weaves together fragments of experience into a tapestry of happiness. The joy isn't just in seeing new sights; it's in finding those unexpected connections that make the world feel both vast and deeply familiar, as though different times, places, and worlds are all coming together in your journey.

During my free time when I'm not travelling, you'll often find me gazing at the sky, losing myself in a good book, or soaking in the beauty of nature. I've always had a soft spot for sunrises, sunsets, winters, rain, oceans, music, and all the wonderful melodies nature shares with us. Once, someone shared a beautiful thought with me that God has gifted humans with an extraordinary ability to give and receive love. And, this tremendous love cannot be caged to just one element—it flows through so many things, like the beauty of nature, the shifting shades of the day, the rhythm of music, and countless other simple joys. That idea has stayed with me, reminding me to cherish the world around me. It's such a simple thing, but it always makes me feel special.

"You know, while gazing at the ocean I strongly feel that we came from the ocean. It's kind of a crazy thought, but we carry salt water within us for whole lives—in our blood, in our cells. So, the sea is basically our first home. Maybe that's why the shore feels so calming.

Standing where the waves break, it's like we're exiles finally coming back to where we belong."

Gazing at the Majestic Ocean, endless sky, and distant mountains has the magical capacity of calming mind. It helps in stepping back from the chaos of daily life and reminds that life is bigger than any one moment. Whether it's a sunny day or a beautiful sunset, just looking up feels like a little escape. It's comforting to know that the vast, open, majestic nature is always there, offering peace and perspective whenever we need it. You might experience something similar when your plane takes off. As it climbs higher, everything below starts to shrink — the buildings, the cars, and even worries. Suddenly, those worries don't feel as big. From up there, the world looks so different, and it's like you can finally see how small some problems really are. That perspective makes me feel lighter, freer, and happier.

Happiness is in a 'Deep Conversation'

"Isn't it the most satisfying feeling when I have stories to tell, and you have time to listen? If your answer is yes, then let's make it happen—pull down the shades, unplug the telephone, set the mobile to flight mode, and just listen. Listen to those soaked thoughts, creative ideas, and pay attention to details of moods, expressions – be 'all ears'.

Stories can weave the world together. Can't they? They hold pieces of my heart, my mind, and my soul, ready to share with you. Some stories will make you laugh; others might bring a tear to your eye. They are not just words but echoes of moments lived, emotions felt, and dreams imagined. All they need is your presence—your undivided, cherished presence.

Another most relaxing thing in life is having people you can go to—whether it's family, a close friend, or even someone at work. You know, those people who let you just *be* yourself. No drama, no pretence, no need to filter who you are. You can be as random, as raw, and as unpolished as you want. And you know what's even better? These are the same people who let you share silence, too. No awkwardness, no pressure to fill the quiet—just sitting together, being. That kind of connection is rare, and honestly, it's priceless.

For me, I'm not a "group friend" kind of person. But I have my people—the ones I can turn to when I need to vent, laugh, or simply exist. Finding those people? That's pure bliss. Honestly, I'd count it as one of the greatest treasures of life.

And yes, I've got a lot to share—a few wonderful ideas, some amazing stories, and, of course, plenty of chatterbox moments. Yeah, happiness isn't always about the big, flashy milestones. It's in the small, everyday moments that we sometimes overlook. Like a road trip filled with laughter, a random walk where an old friend shares a memory that takes you back, or even hearing the pure excitement in your child's voice as they tell you about a new book they're reading.

These moments might seem ordinary, but they're the real treasures. They shape the stories of our lives. And just like the sky—vast and interconnected—these stories weave together to form something much bigger. They're part of an ever-evolving narrative that ties us to each other and reminds us of the beauty in simply being present.

So, what do you say? Let's share some stories—or maybe even some silence. Let's find happiness in the little things that make life extraordinary.

Happiness is amid 'Facts and Fantasies'

The fact is that I am broken, and the fantasy is that I will be healed soon. The fact is that it's a horrible moment and the fantasy is that it will not last forever. The fact is that I am suffering in a vacuum and the fantasy is that tremendous love from nature is showering upon me. In yesterday's love moments, I found him embracing, the fact is he is not here today, and the fantasy is that I will meet him in my dreams- uncaged. Well, life is about neither facts nor fantasies. It's rather about swapping one with the other. Trying to relate this to one of my previous 'short' writings-

"The paper on which she wrote her heart was spoiled with the dispersion of ink. This ink was dispersed coz of water droplets fell from her eyes. Almost on the verge of collapse, she was trying hard to survive the most

difficult time of her life. Forbidden from all dimensions of existence, she took pen and paper to rescue herself. Her soul was torn, her wounds were open, and her skin was peeled. Her inner self was crushed, shaken, fearful, and insecure, on the brink of suicide, she chose to write. What to do? Where to go? Whom to ask for help? Those thoughts tore up her psyche badly. Amid her endless search for a way out, she bent her head over the table and slipped into sleep, in the hope that perhaps her dream world would take her to a comfort zone."

Well, make use of fantasies when realities are too harsh; and come back to realities when your fantasies are not convenient anymore. Well, life is not only about talking history and finding room for self-improvement, it's also about fantasies, fun and living moments. After all, the very first thing you shall take care of under the sky is 'you' only.

This means you are your first and foremost responsibility. In all weathers of life, you have every right to take care of yourself- your physical, mental, and emotional well-being. So, keep switching your modes between facts and fantasies, to soothe yourself. Right?

But you must know that fantasy is different from daydreaming. While daydreaming is like building castles in the air, fantasies are about your future goals and life dreams. Fantasies could be romantic, professional, and even involve changing your physical appearance drastically or becoming a rock star. Our fantasies really infused us to establish our goals and provide motivation to strive for them.

In some sense, they also form and shape our interpersonal relations under the influence of those fantasies. For instance- a woman tends to get attracted to a man whom she fanaticizes about. I mean she is much more likely to respond to a man of her fantasies who somehow indicates his willingness to meet her fantasy. Likewise, a man is most likely to seek out a woman who reciprocates his fantasies. Maybe they never discuss or are even aware of this subliminal connection, but it certainly exists.

Sometimes, logic can make you feel isolated, as it focuses on facts and reason, which can separate you from others. But fantasies, whether in people or a shared dream, bring people together, making unity feel natural and meaningful, even when things don't always make sense.

In a quite similar way, we interact with family, friends, spouses, or strangers; set our targets for life; prefer any political leader, and make investment decisions. For young and growing children particularly, it is one of the essential parts of their development process which they imbibe and grow with. Then there is a gradual modification in this thing, as the age grows. Older people still fantasize about reliving their past or about the overall goodness of life.

Yes, we all can fantasize in one way or another, yet there is a good variety. I am sure that you must be able to relate to these views while recalling your fantasies. A few might be running parallel to this text. Ok. Now, we have arrived at the point that facts are good and fantasies too are. I mean we can jump between them whenever we should. However, there is a big no to situations like all fantasies, no reality, and all reality, no fantasies. Impact-fully, we can live somewhere in between them with the right checks and balances to have a fulfilled life.

The pressure to always be happy can feel overwhelming. We often think happiness is something to chase and hold onto, but it's not that simple. Happiness isn't a constant state; it's fleeting, messy, and often comes in various shapes and sizes. It's found in the moments.

"Happiness is solace and nature."
"Happiness is waking up to your loved ones."
"Happiness is about dreaming."
"Happiness is dancing in the rain."
"Happiness is finding meaning."
"Happiness is staying messy, random, and raw."
"Happiness is acceptance and gratitude."
"Happiness is the smell of freshly brewed coffee."
"Happiness is losing yourself in a good book."
"Happiness is a child's laughter echoing in the air."
"Happiness is feeling the warmth of the sun on your face."

Instead of constantly trying to be happy, I've learned to embrace life's ups and downs and understood that it's also okay to 'not feel happy' all the time. It's not at all equating to endorsing sadness but it's actually letting go of the pressure to be happy all the time, and to focus on the moments that make life feel real—whether they're good, bad, or somewhere in between. True happiness isn't just about reaching the final destination; it's also about the journey. More so, it's about living authentically, finding joys, appreciating the little things, and accepting your authentic self.

CHAPTER 5
THE SCIENCE BEHIND CHOOSING VALUES

Chapter 5
The Science Behind Choosing Values

Papers were scattered in the room like those words, those wounds. They were there, and they were here. Look! They were talking, playing, and creating new stories, talks, and melodies. I was simply watching them subtly expressing themselves as if they knew it all and were the world in themselves. Ah! There was quite a decent noise in the room caused by these pages of a story - somewhat written, and somewhat not. By this time my mother entered the room and lowered the speed of the ceiling fan. "Hey! Why don't you get them bound? Get up, organize these pages, and get them tied", my mother questioned. "Together they will look better and carry some sense rather than these scattered pieces," she continued. I was still in that mosaic of sounds they created together, watching one page being placed over the other in random order. Yes, there was a sequence in this story, but does life have a sequence? Do our beliefs, priorities, and values have any sequence? I wondered whether my life was just in the right order.

Well, we all can get a lot of books, editorials, columns, and cover stories navigating each decade of life with a purpose but to be true, nothing really fits in. We may find tons of literature on 'How to spend your life in your - 20s, 30s, 40s, and 50s to 60s and even beyond'. But it may not truly happen and we shall have to take chances with different career choices, philosophies, and lifestyles to make or unmake ourselves. Alongside, the rough sketch of our life's masterpiece is well embedded with values but they also keep changing. At one point, we may prioritize one value over the other and vice versa. Yeah, we keep refining our life's values and structure by trimming what doesn't work and strengthening what does. Herein, values become our torch-bearers.

Values help us decide what is important in life. If understood scientifically, values are those positive or negative emotions that formulate psychology, attach identity, and greatly influence the behaviour of individuals, societies, and nations.

Quite often, we see value dichotomy inside, and outside us. At display, there are plenty of good values that we often choose to measure and compare ourselves to like a measuring stick to determine a successful and meaningful life on earth. In routine life, we often struggle to choose one value over the other or try to fix the right combination of a few 'good' values and spend a lot of time with it. Something like- nurturing human relationships- can be a good value, but does it hold well for your life every time? May not necessarily. Similarly, values like honesty, integrity, benevolence, wisdom, righteousness, respect etc. are usually considered good, but can they all be your core values to chase? I don't know. Similarly, insult, oppression, aggression, avoiding responsibilities, feeling super good all the time, killing innocent creatures, and not loving your nation, are some less admired values. But at one time or another, you encounter them. Agreed?

They say a great value system is like a compass that keeps telling us the direction and way forward in life. Umm, I am not consuming it. I want to explore further on this stance. For instance, let's assume that you want to succeed at 'any cost' and are aligning all your values to achieve your goals. You are working hard, maintaining discipline, managing time properly, practising perseverance, setting boundaries and acting with all discipline to achieve it. But what if your definition of success is horrific - like say crushing people, slaughtering millions, terrorising nations, and dominating the world? Then all that hard work and discipline will go towards demented and destructive aims.

This dichotomy reflects that though values act like a compass that can show us the direction but at the same time, they cannot tell us whether the direction is right or wrong. When values like discipline, hard work, and boundary-setting are aligned with harmful or destructive goals, the results can indeed be catastrophic. History offers examples of individuals and groups who adhered to such value systems to achieve horrifying ends.

Members of terrorist organisations are highly disciplined in their operations. They manage territories, implement governance, and use technology to spread propaganda. Their value system includes unwavering loyalty to their ideology, rigorous training, and a sense of purpose. However, their definition of success involves acts of terrorism, genocide, and oppression. More so, Adolf Hitler exemplified discipline, vision, and focus. He effectively used propaganda, managed a vast military machine, and rallied an entire nation behind his ideology. However, his definition of success involved racial purity, territorial domination, and the extermination of millions of people, resulting in the Holocaust and World War II. Even so, certain political leaders and regimes prioritize loyalty, discipline, and economic growth, yet achieve these ends through suppression of dissent, exploitation, and human rights abuses.

It means a value system alone doesn't guarantee ethical outcomes. It's the underlying definition of success and the moral framework that guides these values which determine whether the direction is constructive or destructive.

A value system without a grounding in empathy, respect for others, and the greater good can lead to disastrous consequences. Values need to be anchored with the moral and ethical foundation of that system along with introspection and alignment of values. A compass may show the way, but it's up to the traveller to decide if the destination is worth reaching. What are your thoughts?

We Do Both - Chose and Chase - Values

Choosing values is a conscious, deliberate process. It's about identifying what resonates with you on a fundamental level and selecting values that align with your true self and your long-term goals. For example, you might choose values like integrity, family, or kindness because they reflect your core beliefs and purpose in life. When you choose values, you're setting a foundation that guides your decisions, actions, and relationships. For example, you choose the value of work-life balance because you understand it's essential for your well-being and family life, and you prioritize it over a career that demands excessive time away from home.

Chasing values, on the other hand, is often reactive or driven by external pressures, desires, or fleeting circumstances. It's about pursuing values that might seem desirable in the moment, but they may not always align with your true self or long-term fulfilment. Chasing values can lead to a sense of dissatisfaction or a feeling of always striving for something that doesn't quite feel right. For example, you might chase the value of status or wealth because society or your peer group places high importance on it, even though it doesn't truly bring you fulfilment or align with your deeper sense of purpose.

As we grow, we do both—choose and chase. Initially, we may choose values that align with our deeper purpose, but as we evolve, we might chase new values that reflect our changing circumstances, desires, and experiences.

When I was in love, I wanted to get married to him, and at that time, 'love' was the value that I placed above all other values. I remember the early days of being in love when everything else seemed secondary. Love was my compass, my driving force. But once the honeymoon phase of marriage gave way to the everyday reality of bills, work, and dreams deferred, ambition crept back into the forefront. I started missing a 'sense of purpose' in life and desired to chase my career. Then, the 'ambition', and 'aspiration' replaced the 'love' and put it somewhere at 2nd place. I am sure, many of us can relate to this. Can't you?

Knowingly or unknowingly, we all keep interacting and resonating through our values in many ways. Certainly, one value never remains always at the top, though we can still keep that in the top 5 or 10. Studies say that humans are wired to have two sets of values- core values and secondary values. The first one is either permanent or will stay for a prolonged time in our lives, and the second is likely to shift with a change in situation or circumstances.

Remember, nothing in the universe is entirely repeated. Everything is overtly or subtly different in at least some precise way. Here to find out how one is different, one shall follow their own individual instincts to recognize, revise, and reconcile the meaningful variations that occur in lives in different phases. Means, our needs, orientations and purposes shift in life and we tend to choose values that support our purpose. Putting it the other way around, our purposes are need-based, and needs are changing constantly. Does that mean values too are changing? For a few- absolutely yes! And, for another few- partially yes! Seems scientifically logical? See, how our experiences, life episodes and major learnings evolve us as human beings, and on our way, we drop or pick certain values. It occurs to us naturally. And, in this process, a few of our core values remain relatively stable for a prolonged life-time but we also host a few secondary values that are likely to shift and change very quickly.

Now, this constant flux in values and purposes doesn't mean we're lost; it means we're alive. I remember when I was younger, my most cherished value was curiosity. I'd spend hours sitting with my grandfather to hear his stories, asking questions or reading books. Back then, knowledge felt like the only thing that mattered. But as I grew older and faced the competitive grind of life, ambition quietly took its place. My goals became sharper, and my curiosity—though still there—took a backseat to deadlines, achievements, and proving myself. I didn't even notice when that shift happened;

it was subtle, like pages rearranging themselves in the story I was writing.

Even love—so pure and powerful—shifts in life. It isn't that love disappears; it simply moves to a quieter, more stable corner of our hearts. It's still there, like a page we can always return to, but it may no longer remain the title of our stories.

And, then there are times when our values clash. Like when I had to choose between staying late at work to meet a crucial deadline or going home to spend time with my family. I told myself I valued family, but in those moments, my actions often betrayed me. I'd choose the deadline, convincing myself it was "for them." But was it? Or was it just ambition demanding its due? It's hard to say. The guilt would settle in quietly, like an unread page of the story, nagging at me to rewrite it.

What I've learned is that life doesn't demand perfection or consistency from us—it demands presence- the presence of thoughts, actions and moves. Of course, rightly toned!

It's not about clinging to a single value for life or feeling guilty when one value outweighs another. It's about recognizing the shifts, embracing them, and asking ourselves honestly- *Will this shift serve me?*

Some pages of our story may never be complete, and that's okay. Others will be rewritten or torn out altogether. What matters is that we keep writing, keep choosing, and keep questioning. So, when my mother told me to bind those scattered pages, she wasn't just talking about tidying up. She was reminding me to create meaning—to take the chaos of my life, my choices, and my values, and weave them into something that feels true.

Not perfect, not permanent, but true. And maybe that's all we can ever hope for is to live authentically, with our values as both compass and guide, even as the winds of life change their direction.

Protecting Values or Taking a U-turn

Be it individuals, societies or nations, they all re-evaluate paths, and realign values for the future. It can be either protecting the values or taking a U-turn, the idea is serving the greater good. However, at any level—changing values requires a great amount of courage, introspection, and a willingness to challenge the status quo for the larger purpose. At times, protecting our values feels like holding on to a lifeboat in a storm. But what if the storm changes direction, and the lifeboat no longer takes you where you need to go?

When values were protected-

Liu Xiaobo- a Chinese writer and activist - who stood firm for his values of freedom and justice, even when it came at a great personal cost. He was a key figure behind the *Charter 08* manifesto, which called for an independent legal system, freedom of association, and an end to one-party rule in China. In 2009, Liu was arrested and sentenced to 11 years in prison for "inciting subversion of state power." Even while in prison, his commitment to non-violence and human rights earned him the 2010 Nobel Peace Prize. He became the first Chinese citizen to win the prize while living in China and one of only a few people in history to receive it while in detention. Liu chose to stand by his values, no matter how difficult the journey was.

Roxana Saberi- an American journalist, was arrested in Iran and held for 100 days after being falsely accused of espionage. She had been living in Iran for six years, researching for a book that aimed to offer a balanced view of Iranian society. Under intense pressure and threats of a long prison sentence or even execution, Roxana falsely confessed to being a spy. But soon, she realized her mistake and recanted, even though it meant risking her freedom. Instead of being freed, her case went to trial, and she was sentenced to eight years in prison.

"I would rather tell the truth and stay in prison than tell lies to be free," Roxana said, showing her commitment to her values.

During her time in prison, Roxana went on a hunger strike, surviving only on water with sugar. After two weeks, her lawyer appealed her conviction, and an appeals court reduced her sentence to a two-year suspended term, leading to her release. Roxana protected her values, even in the face of great adversity. As she said, "Maybe other people can hurt my body, but they can't hurt my soul unless I let them."

Malala Yousafzai- a Nobel Peace Prize winner who survived an assassination attempt by the Taliban, in Pakistan for advocating girls' education. Rather than succumbing to fear, she pivoted from being a local activist to a global advocate for education and human rights. Her decision to amplify her mission on an international scale—despite the risks—made her the youngest recipient of the Nobel Peace Prize and a symbol of resilience. Despite adverse situations, she protected her values and turned her personal trauma into global advocacy with courage and clarity.

When values were shifted-

In her twenties, Michelle Obama – who served as the first lady of the USA from 2009 to 2017, was climbing the ladder of success as a corporate lawyer, a role that promised prestige and financial rewards. Yet, as she candidly wrote in *Becoming*, she found herself empty, realizing that the path she was on didn't align with the deeper sense of purpose she craved. The glitter of the corporate world didn't match the fulfilment she sought. After a lot of soul-searching, patience, and weighing the costs—like sacrificing a higher salary for a more meaningful job—she took a bold U-turn. Leaving behind the corporate boardrooms, she moved into public service, first with the Chicago mayor's office and later with a non-profit organisation dedicated to empowering young people from underprivileged backgrounds. Michelle called that role the greatest job she ever had, showing us that sometimes, veering off the path we thought was meant for us can lead to something far more rewarding. It's a reminder that values evolve, and the courage to change course can bring us closer to our true purpose.

Now, I will tell you about another interesting U-Turn by a renowned Professor Brian Cox. You might imagine yourself in a rock band while sitting through a physics class, but for Professor Cox, it was the opposite. He- who swapped the thrill of performing on stage for the profound Musician and a Professor- has a striking story of how values can evolve, even leading to a complete U-turn in life. In the 1980s and '90s, Cox was living the dream of many- touring as a keyboardist in the pop bands Dare and D:Ream, even scoring a number- one hit with *Things Can Only Get Better*. Yet, despite the glitz and glamour of the music world, Cox found himself daydreaming about something else— science. Rather than chasing pop stardom, Cox made a bold decision to follow his true calling. While on one tour, he started reading science books, and after five years in the music industry, he made a radical shift. He enrolled at the University of Manchester to study physics and eventually became a professor of particle physics. Cox reassessed his priorities. For him, the allure of music was eventually overshadowed by the pull of the universe's mysteries, showing that sometimes, what we think we want isn't what we're truly meant to do.

Amrita Sher-Gil, one of India's greatest modern artists, initially trained in European art styles in Paris and turned from European Modernist to Indian Traditionalist on her return to India in the 1930s. Inspired by Indian traditions and rural life, she shifted her focus to capturing the essence of India's cultural and social landscapes, blending her Western techniques with a uniquely Indian perspective.

Further, Germany as a nation, after the devastation of World War II, made a critical U-turn in its values. Rejecting the ideologies of the Nazi regime, the country embraced democracy, human rights, and international cooperation. Initiatives such as the Marshall Plan, reconciliation with Holocaust survivors, and reparations to affected nations were part of this transformation. Germany's U-turn became a model for national accountability and reconstruction, showing the world that even after immense wrongdoing, a country can choose a path of healing and progress. This reflects that the U-turn was better when existing values were not serving the greater good.

Knowingly or unknowingly, we all either protect our values or get swayed away from them. I remember a friend of mine, who always believed honesty was her most sacred value. She prided herself on her ability to speak her mind, no matter the situation. But one day, during a sensitive work meeting, her unfiltered honesty backfired. A casual remark she made about a colleague's work ethic strained relationships within the team. That experience made her question her rigid adherence to honesty above all else. It wasn't that honesty wasn't important—it just needed to be tempered with empathy and timing. She learned that sometimes, protecting a value doesn't mean sticking to it blindly; it means adapting it to fit the bigger picture.

Authentic or In-Authentic Self and Values

Human beings are clever creatures. We can blend positive and negative values in our minds and find intelligent ways to justify our behavior using self-serving interpretations of the given reality. Though no one is absolutely – right or wrong, even though we practice self-deception as a norm. Or, I can say that we practice, preach and propagate things as we want yet we want to be seen as reasonable.

Imagine Hitler, Stalin, or Mao - would have caused less damage to the world if they had authentically revealed their cruel personal values to the world and would have not justified their brutal behavior according to their own twisted standards. The same holds true in today's money-driven world when the 'ends' are justified, not the means. Irrespective of means people who are able to make money are glorified and celebrated like examples to everyone else.

Human psychology is indeed a web of complex identities, where we constantly form mental images of ourselves and others. When we interact with someone, it's often not the true "us" engaging with the true "them" but rather the version of ourselves we've constructed based on our perceptions and assumptions about them. Your mental images shape the way we communicate and express our values, often leading to behaviours that are more about maintaining these identities than about authentic connection.

Authenticity is a state of true self - including our values- is often expressed through our interactions, judgements, inhibitions and virtues. In reverse, inauthenticity is seen as a character flaw. However, its darker side is contrary to popular belief. Means, pro social and ethical behavior may be found to have been in contrast with authenticity. Politicians often navigate this complexity, balancing personal beliefs with the need to maintain public support. They might pretend to support a policy they don't fully agree with to please voters, compromising their authenticity for the sake of political gain. Herein, pressure to appear virtuous can lead to inauthentic behavior.

This process can feel inauthentic because it's not the raw, unfiltered self-being presented—it's a version shaped by social conditioning, past experiences, and assumptions. When we approach others with preconceived notions about who they are, we often respond in a way that is more about maintaining those images than being genuinely present. For example, you may act more reserved around an authority figure to maintain a professional image, or more playful with a friend because you've internalized that role. This pattern of behaviour, influenced by external factors, can sometimes make us feel inauthentic, and disconnected from our true selves.

"Everyone can act or talk nice coz that's not taxable."

Our lives actually lie somewhere between being authentic or inauthentic. Certainly, our values, and personality types play a major role in representing ourselves differently in different settings. When you're at home surrounded by family or close friends, you might feel completely authentic, allowing yourself to be vulnerable and express your true thoughts and emotions without fear of judgment. In contrast, in a professional setting, you may intentionally present a more polished or controlled version of yourself, aligning with the expectations and roles required in that space. This shift isn't always about deception; it's about adapting to the context. Your personality, whether introverted or extroverted, also shapes this dynamic—making you either more open and expressive or more reserved and cautious in your interactions.

The deeper challenge lies in navigating these various roles without losing touch with your core values and sense of self. It's a delicate dance of balancing authenticity with the need to adapt to social expectations, all while ensuring that each version of yourself remains connected to the essence of who you truly are, regardless of the circumstances.

Values in Tumultuous Relationships

Love is just like sunlight. Love is not a selective value, it's not exclusive, and it's meant for all. However, the intensity with which 'love' can be felt can vary. The bond we share with others isn't just limited to humans alone, we can feel the same connection with nature or animals or even a stranger sitting next. The only difference is how strongly and deeply we feel about them.

Should I stay or should I go? There are moments when life demands a complete U-turn, and that's not even an easy choice. Many times, I have seen people standing at the fork in their relationship on whether to stay or leave. Well, the answer can't be easier and simpler. It's just that you need to be patient, assess the relationship climate, listen to the wisdom of your body, and focus on the collective future. Yeah, but in situations, when the other one has already dumped you, you can't remain stuck with your values anymore. For you to survive, you must stop keeping yourself updated about them, tracing their life and you must also take a U-turn from your old preserved values. It may appear like losing the meaning of life, losing a part of yourself, and experiencing almost a death-like feeling.

More, call it a lost sense of identity or heavy emptiness, a dark black hole inside gets created, without any real purpose. Naturally, humans prefer 'staying in a relationship' over 'staying in opposition' as the latter, takes a lot of physical and mental energy, leaving us drained. Herein, you may desperately try to compromise and fix everything to get back the life that you had. You might have been spending every second, minute, and hour of your day and night overtly thinking about that, shedding tears, and forgetting all other facts. Sad but it's all in vain. Say it coping mechanism or a psychological quirk, a few might even choose to laugh at past misfortunes, turn them into amusement, and gain greater emotional well-being. In fact, those memories are pretty shitty and cause you to remember the life that you want to have right now with no real connection. Simply, you are viewing your past through rose-coloured glass. Trust me, nothing can be moved. The only thing that can fix you is you. No matter what and how things occurred, it's now your responsibility to fix yourself.

Values in Leadership Role

More often than not, being authentic is complete opposite to what a person in a leadership role should be. Yeah, but this doesn't legitimize manipulation or tactics of self-deception. Certainly, not. To be true, it requires a great degree of self-control, and regulation and displaying the best version of yourself. Of course, this would be different from your uncensored, unfiltered and uninhibited version of yourself. Imagine any 'good' leader in and around you who would have been reflecting a repertoire of behaviors for better interpersonal functioning. Most likely, they would speak less, listen more, and understand varied perspectives. So, that empirical and sensible definition of 'authenticity' ought to be well-tempered with the aspirational self. And, of course, 'aspiration' is itself an authentic value!

Last year, I had the privilege of attending a one-week Leadership Development Program at the Indian Institute of Management. In one of the sessions, the instructor, who was the director of IIM, handed us forms containing questions with responses ranging from 1 to 3 marks. After filling them out, we were instructed to plot our responses on a graph to observe the bell curve. Each participant was given nearly an hour for this task. Following its completion, there was a tea break before we reconvened to discuss what the curves represented. However, I had a peculiar reason to worry—my curve was flat, almost resembling a dead patient's heartbeat. Anxious, I approached the director to ask what this might signify. She smiled and asked me to wait until the discussion. After the break, she began by randomly asking five participants about their scores and then pointed to me for mine. Everyone's curves were displayed on the screen, and among them, mine stood out as the flattest.

The speaker then delivered an insightful explanation, likening our curves to the characteristics of five animals that reside within each of us as individuals, professionals, and leaders: the Tiger, Chameleon, Turtle, Eagle, and Salmon (or Selmon).

Tiger: Powerful and courageous, embodying strength, independence, sharp instincts, and focus, though needing to balance decisiveness with empathy.

Chameleon: Adaptive and versatile, seamlessly blending with surroundings while maintaining core values amidst change.

Turtle: Patient, steady, and resilient, exemplifying determination, though sometimes struggling to adapt in fast-paced settings.

Eagle: Visionary and strategic, soaring high with focus and precision, yet requiring flexibility to adjust their approach.

Salmon: Persistent and determined, navigating upstream challenges with resilience and purpose, often prioritizing others over self, which can impact authenticity.

Further, it was explained that how a flat curve indicated a balanced representation of all these traits. While others had peaks and valleys, showing stronger tendencies toward specific traits, my results reflected versatility—a potential strength in leadership. It showed that I might not have extreme inclinations toward any one characteristic but could flexibly adapt to various situations, embodying the right traits as needed.

In our multi-versioned roles, the truth is -

"We can't know everyone

We can't do everything

We can't go everywhere

We, simply, have to pick and choose between good and a little bit better"

Leadership is not about excelling in one quality but blending diverse traits to suit the situation. This perspective has taught me to embrace adaptability while staying authentic. A leader must balance characteristics like strategic vision, adaptability, compassion, introspection, and drive to navigate challenges effectively. Rooted in values, beliefs, and perception, authenticity guides leaders to act with integrity and purpose, fostering meaningful connections and genuine leadership.

Finally, the Collective Wisdom

Values are obviously subjective, though we can still check their mortality and immortality with some degree of objectivity. As a popular belief, we understand that good values generate positive outcomes and bad values generate negative outcomes in life. Though their degree may vary, and also depending on life circumstances, a few may stay, or may end, or alter.

Choosing human values is challenging, often involving tough trade-offs and conflicting priorities. Love and Empathy, for instance, vary with life experiences—some offer emotional comfort, while others provide practical support shaped by hardship. Similarly, environmental debates highlight tensions between economic needs and long-term planetary care. Cultural differences, like views on arranged marriages, and daily dilemmas, such as balancing justice and mercy, show how values can clash and adapt based on context.

These dilemmas remind us that choosing values isn't just an intellectual exercise—it's a deeply human struggle shaped by empathy, context, and the need to find balance. More so, altering a value or taking a U-turn doesn't mean failure; it means having the courage to say, "This isn't working for me anymore," and pivoting toward something that feels more aligned with who you are now. Sometimes, protecting your values means staying the course, and sometimes it means redefining the journey altogether. Both choices require reflection, courage, and the willingness to listen to what life is telling you.

CHAPTER 6
THE HYPES AROUND PERFECTION—
REAL OR SHALLOW?

Chapter 6
The Hypes around Perfection - Real or Shallow?

We all create hype. It's just that some amongst us create bigger hypes than others. Hypes are created mostly around the professions, relationships, wealth, or status of individuals to generate a sense of superiority over others in society. Not surprisingly, I am sure you must have witnessed that hype culture on social media, in the entertainment industry, in box office predictions, brand images, in political campaigns, You Tube videos and even in the product launches. It's a kind of exaggeration or deception bubble that intends to make things attractive, and appealing. Trust me, the marketing world is worth it.

With the point to sell imaginations through storytelling, or conversations, people try to position themselves by making things look cool. Hypes directly affect our judgements and images as they showcase a fabricated image of the person, brand or anything else for that matter. Though, not all hypes are bad, let's navigate through a situation to relate more. A few years ago, a man, let's call him Dr. David, approached me to help his daughter with her studies. Right from the start, he introduced himself as a surgeon at a prestigious hospital in a Metro City, and when he visited me first time with his wife, he'd emphasize this point with great generosity. At first, I didn't question it. I simply agreed to teach his daughter, and everything went smoothly—until it didn't.

Over time, Dr. David would occasionally talk about his daughter's progress, and in these conversations, he'd often share stories about his work also—about surgeries, patients, his tiring days in the operating room, and more. He'd even send pictures, sometimes of blood-stained gloves or his work at the hospital. As things grew, I too began seeking his advice for my family's health issues. I thought I knew him well—he seemed like a generous and hardworking man who had earned himself a place in the society.

That was until one evening when, for no particular reason, I found myself scrolling through LinkedIn. A thought popped into my head to check the hospital website where Dr. David had said he worked. But when I searched the surgeon's list, his name wasn't there. I tried again, more focused this time, and still, no trace of him. This raised my eyebrows, so I decided to dig deeper. I even looked up other hospitals where he claimed to consult, but there was no clue about him. Going further, and to my surprise, I found him on a Professional Networking Website but without the "Dr." as prefix—i.e. not as a surgeon, but as a marketing professional! It took me months to process what I had uncovered.

So, I couldn't help but wonder why people create these elaborate hypes about themselves. Why do they feel the need to project an image that isn't real? The truth behind such behaviour often lies in deeper psychological factors. In marketing, creating hype generates attention, builds excitement, and engages others. Similarly, some people create personal hype to boost their self-image or to gain social acceptance. With co-workers or friends, it often shows up in casual conversations. Someone might sigh dramatically and mention how they're "so exhausted" from juggling endless responsibilities, framing it as a sign of how important they are at work. Or they might say they've been "too swamped with back-to-back calls" with senior management, subtly hinting at their value to the team. Then there are those who weave in personal struggles, sharing how they've had to "overcome so much" to get where they are, turning their challenges into a spotlight moment. It's less about the story itself and more about crafting an image that feels impressive or significant.

Psychologically, this can be linked to the herd mentality, the tendency to follow group norms and seek validation through conformity. In workplaces or social circles where busyness or struggle is seen as a marker of importance, people may feel pressured to create their own hype to fit in. Herein individuals, despite valuing their individuality, subconsciously mimic others to fit in. It's a way to conform to the majority, driven by a fear of rejection or a lack of self-awareness. When people constantly internalize the opinions, feelings, and beliefs of others, they start confusing them with their own, losing touch with their true selves.

Further, another darker side of hype behaviour becomes apparent when individuals mirror the words, gestures, and even postures of those whom they admire or wish to resemble. Psychologists explain that people are naturally inclined to copy the body language, tone, and mannerisms of those around them—often without realizing it—especially when they feel uncertain or inferior. This tendency to mirror others reflects a lack of confidence and an inability to stand firmly in one's own identity. Ultimately, creating hype around one's life or achievements can be a mask for emptiness, an attempt to cover up the discomfort of not fully accepting one's reality. It's a coping mechanism to fill the void of insecurity and fear of being judged, rather than embracing who they truly are.

Let's see if this relates to the idea of Existentialism, particularly the work of Jean-Paul Sartre. Sartre believed that people often create false identities or roles to escape the anxiety and meaninglessness of life. In his view, individuals sometimes cling to social expectations or exaggerated versions of happiness to avoid confronting their true selves. This "bad faith" is a form of self-deception, where people pretend to be something they're not in order to avoid facing their inner struggles or the reality of their existence.

Existentialism, much like Nietzsche's philosophy, emphasizes the importance of authenticity and accepting the full range of human emotions, including pain, doubt, and suffering. True freedom, Sartre argued, comes from facing these uncomfortable truths, embracing our responsibility for our choices, and living in a way that is true to ourselves. This philosophy suggests that clinging to constant happiness or an idealized version of life can be an escape from the more challenging but necessary aspects of existence.

Hype Kills Your Story

People hype to look superior and get exclusive treatment. Doing this probably exempts them from getting scrutinized at least up to a few basic levels. That means now they are not competing at level 0 or level 1 rather, they might be somewhere from level 7 to level 8. Well, it's a kind of trap that people usually fall into pretending to be someone or something that they are not. For instance, pretending to be a happy couple, a rich man, a skilled professional, a great philanthropist, a great listener, or a great son, daughter, or parent, whatnot. Undeniably, social networking websites are excellently doing their job to help people curate their online identity and satisfy their need for self-validation and approval.

"The simply complete thing, then, is that which is always chosen for itself and never on account of something else." — Aristotle

In other words, using these sites people post selected realities about their personal and professional accomplishments even if the grass is not that green. Apparently, a torrent of posts about exotic vacations, glamorous selfies, cheerful get-together portraits, or sports triumphs, hits the nerve. Ironically, many of the happy-looking couples confessed to fighting moment's right before and after the photo, people vacationing solo on exotic locations were dealing with their worst feelings of isolation or depression, or other mental health issues associated with them. To the extent, that a happy and smiling person may have been seeing a devastating time in real life or even at the verge of suicide.

Does hype manipulate our brains?

When someone hypes their identity, it taps into deep-seated psychological triggers that affect how we perceive them and ourselves. This manipulation often leverages the brain's social wiring, where we are hardwired to seek approval, validation, and connection. The person hyping their identity may present themselves as exceptional, unique, or highly desirable, triggering our brain's social comparison system. We begin to compare ourselves to their elevated self-image, which can lead to feelings of admiration, envy, or a desire to be part of their "exclusive" group. This plays into the halo effect, where we attribute positive qualities to someone based on a few standout traits or achievements they've emphasized.

Moreover, by constantly emphasizing their identity, they build a sense of self-worth based on how others see them, encouraging people to view them in the same way. The brain responds to this continuous reinforcement by associating their identity with social status and relevance. This creates a feedback loop, where both the person hyping themselves and their audience feel a sense of connection, status, and recognition. The manipulation is subtle but powerful. It can lead to a shift in how we perceive the person, making us more likely to admire, follow, or even adopt similar traits in our own lives.

Hype Vs Play-down

When we talk about personality, we often focus on how people present themselves to the world. Are they extroverted or introverted? Confident or reserved? Role models or self-centred? But the truth is, most of us have two sides to our personality- the one we show to others and the one that reflects our deeper, internal needs. Striking a balance between these sides is where the challenge lies, and this is where the concepts of hype and play-down personalities come into play.

One of my schoolmates, Arjun, is now a software engineer at a tech company in Chennai. He's always been the quiet achiever, consistently delivering results without seeking the spotlight. He'd quietly fix issues behind the scenes, the one people turned to when things went wrong. But Arjun was never one to hype himself up. He believed that results spoke louder than words, so he kept a low profile, letting his work do the talking. Then came Priya, his colleague who was a complete opposite. Confident, loud, and always ready to share her wins, Priya made sure everyone knew what she was up to. She updated her social media with every project, posted her successes, and made sure she was visible in the office. Arjun, despite working just as hard, couldn't help but feel overshadowed. It was hard to ignore how much attention Priya was getting, while his own efforts seemed to go unnoticed.

It was during a team meeting that Arjun's manager, Ravi, said something that stuck with him: "Arjun, you're doing great work, but I don't hear about it enough. We need to make sure people know what you're contributing." That's when Arjun realized something crucial that in today's world, it's not just about doing great work, and it's about making sure people see it. He understood that no matter how hard you work, if you don't make an effort to be visible, it's like your contributions don't even exist. It wasn't about hyping or playing down; it was about ensuring your hard work didn't go unnoticed. It was about balancing both aspects.

"You know what the best jobs of the industry don't go to the best candidates. Rather, they go to the best job seekers. And, these best job seekers may not even have the relevant job experiences for the job, but they simply are captivating communicators who never overestimate whom they are talking to."

Well, it's a fine line between hyping yourself up and playing down your achievements. Arjun had always downplayed his success, but sometimes, you need to speak up and let people know what you're doing. In a world where visibility often equals recognition, you can't afford to stay silent about your accomplishments. You don't need to shout about it, but also don't be afraid to share your wins and ensure your efforts are seen.

Hype personalities thrive on standing out. They highlight their successes, amplify their presence, and project an image of confidence and achievement. Think of celebrities like Kim Kardashian or Elon Musk, who use social media to build larger-than-life personas. Their hype helps them capture attention and admiration, but it can also create pressure to maintain an idealized image, even if it doesn't align with who they truly are.

I've seen this on a personal level, too—like a friend who constantly talks about their achievements but later confides that they rely on external validation to feel secure. On the other hand, play-down personalities prefer a more understated approach. They let their actions speak louder than their words and often avoid the spotlight. While this can feel authentic and grounded, it sometimes causes their talents to go unnoticed.

Many times, I too get that feeling of holding back, especially when it comes to ambition. It's like, I know what I want, but there's this hesitation to fully own it, like I'm somehow not supposed to. It's not just me—

many people, especially those with a "downplay" personality, often find themselves doing the same thing. We downplay our desires, achievements, or ambitions because we don't want to come across as self-centred or boastful.

Psychiatrist Anna Fels touched on this in her book *Necessary Dreams: Ambition in Women's Changing Lives*. She interviewed a group of highly educated women, and despite their qualifications, none of them would openly admit to being ambitious. They saw ambition as something selfish or manipulative, almost like it was at odds with being humble. Fels pointed out that this reluctance to embrace ambition wasn't just a social convention—it's something deeper, especially because men don't seem to shy away from declaring their ambition. It's like society has placed this unspoken pressure on women (and others with a downplay personality) to keep their ambitions in check, as if wanting more means you're somehow less likeable or less genuine.

I had a student in my class who was smart, hardworking, and had everything going for him. But despite his qualities, he still felt inferior because he didn't have the same things as his peers. He rode a simple two-wheeler, and had a basic phone, while everyone else flaunted fancy cars and the latest iPhones. It made him feel like he wasn't as successful. That, so-called - "iPhone Syndrome" exemplifies how hype and the pressure to conform to certain personalities play out. For some, owning an expensive brand like an iPhone,

Air Jordans, or Gucci is more than just a product—it's a way to show off status and fit in. Social media only adds fuel to the fire, with people posting pictures of their luxury items to signal success or just to keep up with trends. But here's the catch. This constant need to keep up with the hype often creates a lot of pressure—financially and emotionally—to keep upgrading or maintaining a certain image. On the other hand, there are those who avoid flaunting brands or go for more practical choices. They may not focus on material possessions, but they still feel the weight of societal expectations.

Ultimately, both hype and play-down approaches come with their own challenges. While hype personalities may risk losing themselves under the weight of external expectations, play-down personalities may find their efforts going unnoticed, even if they are working just as hard. The key lies in striking a balance between visibility and authenticity.

True self-worth isn't defined by the image we project or the recognition we seek—it's about being genuine in what we do and who we are. Whether it's sharing your accomplishments or quietly working behind the scenes, the important thing is to stay true to yourself. Recognize your values, own your achievements, and don't be afraid to share them in a way that feels authentic to you. Success isn't about shouting the loudest or fading into the background—it's about making sure your contributions are seen for what they truly are.

Imperfection is OK

Have you too ever felt like creating hype? Or chasing a perfect life? Have you ever felt like you're pretending to be someone you're not? Maybe it's at work, with friends, or online. Most of us do it because we're chasing this idea of a perfect life—one where everything is just right.

For most of us, that "perfect" life might look like waking up next to a loving, fit partner, having polite kids, running a successful business, living in a big house, driving fancy cars, and maybe even owning a private island. "If I just had all that," you might think, "I'd be truly happy." It's a tempting thought, isn't it? But let's pause for a second—does it really work that way? There's nothing wrong with dreaming big or wanting more for yourself. The problem starts when we think our happiness depends on having these things. And honestly, it's not really our fault also.

We live in a world that constantly reminds us we're not enough. Ads, influencers, and social media around us—they're all saying, "You need this to be happy," or "You're missing out if you don't have that." People even in casual conversations push this idea that happiness is tied to the things we own. "Get this gadget, and your life will change!" or "Buy this, and you'll finally feel complete." But does it ever last? Think about the last time you bought something you really wanted. How long did that happiness stick around? A week? A month? It probably faded sooner than you'd like to admit.

"Imperfection inspires invention, imagination, creativity. It stimulates. The more I feel imperfect, the more I feel alive."

So, we end up chasing stuff after stuff to feel so-called 'perfect'. We buy new clothes, upgrade our phones, or try to keep up with trends. And for a moment, it feels good. But that feeling doesn't last, does it? It fades quickly, and we're back to square one, looking for the next thing. The truth is, these things would never make you perfect and hence, the happiness tied to things doesn't last. It's like trying to fill a bucket with a hole in it. No matter how much you pour in, it'll never be full.

Maybe it's time to stop and think—what really makes me happy? Is the "perfect happy life" even possible? And is failure really a folly? Am I confusing pleasure with happiness?

The truth is, real happiness isn't about having everything or achieving some idealized version of life. It's about finding joy in the imperfect moments, in the ups and downs, and in simply being yourself. Happiness isn't something you buy or achieve—it's something you experience and appreciate in everyday moments. So, maybe instead of chasing perfection, we should focus on what truly brings us peace and contentment. After all, life's beauty often lies in its imperfections.

Realism and Perfection

Realism is something we live in every day, even if we don't realize it. It's in the way we wake up and face the small struggles—like getting through a tough day at work or juggling family responsibilities. It's about accepting the unfiltered version of life with all its ups and downs, rather than chasing some perfect, ideal version of it.

The idea of Realism is not new. As an art movement, it began in 19th-century France, inspired by this same approach to life. During these times, the Industrial Revolution changed the lives of many, especially the working class. As more people faced hard, everyday realities—working long hours in factories or living in poverty—Realism in art mirrored these struggles. People began to reject the idealized, romanticized portrayals of life and instead wanted art that reflected their own experiences. Artists like Courbet and Millet painted the lives of peasants and labourers in a way that resonated with the reality many people were living.

Artists and writers began showing the world as it truly was—not idealized, not overly emotional, but real. They moved away from styles like Neoclassicism, which focused on perfection and grandeur, and Romanticism, which leaned into dramatic, emotional storytelling. Instead, Realism focused on ordinary people and their everyday lives, even when those lives were messy, flawed, or difficult.

Along the same lines, films and TV shows have moved away from portraying perfect, flawless characters and instead embraced more authentic, complex ones over time. Movies like The Pursuit of Happiness, and Forrest Gump focus on real, relatable struggles—poverty, personal loss, and finding meaning in a messy world. These stories resonate with audiences because they reflect the truth of human experience, rather than a fairy tale or idealized narrative. Also, in *Eat Pray Love*, Julia Roberts' character takes a journey of self-discovery after her divorce. Initially, she seeks happiness in relationships, success, and material possessions—the typical markers of a "perfect" life. However, her path leads her to a profound realization that happiness begins with self-acceptance and inner peace, not external perfection. Her journey illustrates that fixing what's within is far more meaningful than creating an illusion of perfection on the outside. I read this text somewhere and found it so relevant-

"To be considered a desirable woman, the pressure feels endless. You're expected to have every part of your body waxed, get weekly manicures, and wear heels every day. You should look like a Victoria's Secret Angel, even if you work in an office. Being an average-sized woman with natural hair and a simple sweater just doesn't seem enough. We're constantly reminded that our worth is tied to an image, as if we need to live up to an ideal one that was never meant for us."

More so, society has started questioning the "perfect" body image, like the idealized Barbie doll figure. Movements like #BodyPositivity and campaigns from brands like Dove and Aerie, which feature diverse body types and unretouched images, challenge unrealistic beauty standards. These shifts reflect the ongoing influence of Realism, which has always reminded us that there's beauty in the truth of life, no matter how imperfect it may seem. Realism encourages us to find meaning and connection in the real world around us, embracing imperfections and rejecting the pressure to meet unrealistic expectations.

As a way of life, this approach offers an alternative by celebrating the rawness of life and focusing on personal growth. Further, it reminds us that happiness is found not in perfection, but in embracing life's messiness and focusing on what truly matters—our journey, growth, and inner peace.

Perception Is 'Not Always' a Reality

Hype is often used to control perception, making us appear more impressive or valuable, driven by the fear of judgment.

Perception isn't always the same as reality. Our senses can be wrong, and different people may interpret what they see, hear, taste, or feel in different ways. That's why we can't always trust one thought or conclusion. Our thoughts are often uncertain and relative, and we are always somewhat distant from the truth.

In 2014, Robin Williams, the beloved comedian and actor, known for making people laugh, for bringing joy to millions died. Behind his infectious smile and quick wit, he faced a struggle that many never saw. Society had certain expectations of him – to always be the life of the party, to maintain the image of the funny, and happy guy. He was, after all, a public figure, someone whose job was to entertain and make others feel good. The pressure to constantly live up to this perception, to meet the expectations of happiness and success, made him empty from the inside. In reality, Williams was battling severe depression, anxiety, and substance abuse. The persona he had to uphold for the world was far different from the inner turmoil that created a sharp divide between his public and private life. And, it grew harder for him to fit into a mould that others had created for him, contributing to his tragic death by suicide in 2014. Williams' story reminds us that when we allow perception to define us, when we live for others' expectations, it can rob us of the space to be our authentic selves—and sometimes, that comes at a heart-breaking cost.

"People's views of us are shaped by what they see on the surface, not by the full depth of who we are."

In 2017, we lost one of our loved one. Like a few of us, he had a history of a few unsuccessful business ventures. For him, getting himself merged into mainstream society after a few failures was quite challenging. Whenever he tried to merge back, people would laugh at him for his past mistakes, label him as a 'loser' and remind him of what went wrong in his 'last try.' It felt like the weight of everyone's judgment crushed him. No matter how hard he worked to change, no matter how many steps he took toward improving, and making a comeback, the perception people had of him never shifted. They only saw the past, the mistakes, and not the person he was trying to become. He tried, I could see that. But every time he reached out, the world seemed to push him back, as if his history defined him more than his present-day efforts. Beneath all this perception, he was a gentleman who had made sacrifices, spread tremendous love, gave all-weather support, and would go to all possible limits to be there for anyone around him. I wish he hadn't cared so much about what society thought of him. I wish he could've blocked out those voices that only focused on his mistakes and just lived for himself. He deserved to find peace in his own progress, and in fact, we all deserve to embrace our journeys without feeling like we have to meet other people's expectations. It breaks my heart to think that if he could've just let go of their opinions, maybe he could've truly found himself again. But the reality is, that the world often doesn't allow that space for change. And, the painful truth is that we lost him.

In 2019, V.G. Siddhartha, the founder of Café Coffee Day (CCD), often referred to as the "Starbucks of India," took his life under heavy societal pressures and expectations. From humble beginnings, he grew CCD into a leading coffeehouse chain, with thousands of outlets across the country. However, behind the public success, Siddhartha faced significant personal and financial struggles and was reportedly under immense pressure to meet the expectations of investors, creditors, and the public. On the contrary, his wife, Malavika Hegde, took a different path after him. In the face of overwhelming adversity, she embraced her role as the leader of Café Coffee Day and worked tirelessly. Instead of being crushed by the pressure to meet others' expectations, Malavika focused on her own vision for the company, making bold decisions and driving the brand forward. Her journey shows that, while society may place heavy burdens on us, it's possible to rise above and redefine success on our own terms. Malavika didn't let the perception of loss and failure define her or the company. Instead, she chose to embrace the challenge, stay authentic, and take the business to new heights without being afraid of how others perceive it.

Herein the important lesson is don't let the fear of perception define you—be authentic and true to yourself, no matter what the world thinks. Don't be afraid of perception. It's easy to get caught up in how others see us, to worry about their judgments, their expectations, and how we measure up. But the truth is, perception is just that—a viewpoint, not the absolute reality. If you let that define you, you're letting someone else write your story. The reality is, that no one else's perception should have the power to hold you back. Be bold in showing who you truly are. Don't be afraid to pursue your dreams, make mistakes, and grow. Let go of the fear of judgment and embrace the freedom to be authentic. The only perception that truly matters is the one you have of yourself. Once you stop fearing what others think, you'll be free to create your own path, regardless of all the labels others try to place on you.

CHAPTER 7

I WANT SUCCESS BUT SUCCESS DOESN'T WANT ME

Chapter 7
I Want Success But Success Doesn't Want Me

What is success? The answer varies for everyone. For some, its wealth; for others, recognition. Years ago, as I sat on a staircase picking flecks of rubble from the carpet, success meant having a warm office job. Over time, my horizons shifted, and success became about money and status. Today, success is also about being a good mother to my son and being there for my parents. Success isn't fixed; it's a continuum, where achieving one goal leads to new aspirations- best illustrated by Maslow's hierarchy of needs theory.

Often, we think, "I want success, but it often feels like it doesn't want me back." Perhaps because we seek it in ways that don't align with who we are or what we truly want.

Herein, I will explore the varied versions of success, starting with examples of hollow pursuits and I'll then touch on the importance of failure and struggle. From there, I'll transition into its elusive nature and conclude with the core idea. Let's begin-

The Hollow Pursuit of Success: Nick's Story

One of my known people, I'll name him Nick, here, is a very enthusiastic man. He wants to win, rule, and then crush the entire world. Not just this, he keeps jumping from one high to another high in life. Always on a high ride, he would push himself in all extreme situations like cracking tough deals, throwing money, randomly shopping, suddenly booking flights, or even, sleeping with any next woman he could found. To many of us, he is perceived as any random guy who would do anything that he wishes to do. No time taking, and no thoughtfulness. Thankfully, he is a blessed man with a lot of family assets and yes, he himself is also able to make a lot of money by fair or unfair means.

You know, anyone could dream of having a carefree life like his—where everything seems so effortless, where random abilities and opportunities seem to fall into his lap. I too once thought the same, imagining how amazing it would be to live with that kind of freedom and endless possibilities. But when I finally met him in person, the reality was far more complex than I had anticipated. What I found was an enthusiastic, passionate man—someone who seemed full of energy and drive. Yet, beneath the surface, there was a darker, shallower side to him that wasn't immediately visible.

Despite having access to anything he could imagine, from wealth to choices, Nick remained a deeply unhappy and dissatisfied person. He had everything most people dream of, but still, there was this void in him that he couldn't fill. It was as though no matter what he achieved, it was never enough. His life was consumed by a constant longing for more—more success, more freedom, and more experiences. But it was never about true fulfilment. He was always searching for something just out of reach, always moving from one fleeting desire to the next, hoping that the next thing would give him the happiness and satisfaction he so desperately craved.

Achieving success is much easier when you know what success looks like. What Nick failed to realize was that his constant need for more had stripped him of authenticity. His personality, instead of growing deeper with wisdom and purpose, had become shallow and ungrounded. He never felt truly successful, never felt successful. This inability to feel content, no matter how much he had, kept him stuck in a cycle of dissatisfaction. He missed the point of what real success was. It wasn't about accumulating things or experiences—it was about finding purpose, peace, and inner contentment.

Nick was seldom stable, calm, or composed. His emotions swung between temporary victories and deep emptiness. Success remained elusive, always just out of reach, despite his material gains. Despite his achievements and fleeting pleasures, he never found lasting fulfilment. His idea of success wasn't about enjoying a contented life or his possessions; it was about ruling others, crushing competitors, and asserting his dominance. For him, success meant proving superiority, no matter the destruction he left in his wake. His inability to appreciate his accomplishments kept him trapped in a cycle of highs and lows, never truly at peace with himself. It reflects the emptiness that comes from chasing external validation, dominance, and superficial success. Perhaps stability in his thoughts, permanence in his relationships, and a deeper sense of purpose could have helped him.

Failure Is Truly Essential

Imagine a life where failure doesn't exist. No mistakes, no setbacks, no problems. At first glance, it might seem ideal—a life free from challenges. But in reality, such a life would be dull, devoid of meaning, and lacking excitement. Without failure, there would be no stories of triumph, no growth, and no moments of self-discovery. Life would be like a never-ending flat line, without the highs and lows that make it worth living. The truth is, that failure helps us understand what success really means. It gives us the strength to keep going, even when things get tough. The greatest stories are often born from the deepest struggles.

In 7th grade, I read Emily Dickinson's poem "Success is Counted Sweetest," and it has stayed with me ever since. At the age of 12 or 13, we were introduced to a critical life lesson- the idea that challenges and struggles give meaning to success. The poem boldly asserts that success is best understood by those who have faced failure. It suggests that it's through adversity that we come to appreciate life's achievements.

Yet, society often sends a contradictory message. In our careers, relationships, exams, and life as a whole, winning is celebrated, while losing feels like an unforgivable offence. From an early age, we're taught that failure is something to avoid at all costs—that "you can't afford to fail." Success is glorified as the ultimate goal, while failure is viewed as a blemish on one's character or reputation.

This mind set permeates every aspect of life, shaping our smallest daily actions and largest ambitions. We become obsessed with success, making failure seem unthinkable. But failure is, in fact, a natural and essential part of life. It often serves as the catalyst for growth, learning, and even greater achievements. By embracing failure, we unlock the potential to truly savour success, much like Dickinson's timeless words remind us.

Everywhere we look—especially on social media—we're surrounded by picture-perfect moments and stories of effortless achievements. But chasing success can feel more like a burden than a blessing. It makes us afraid to fail, smothers our creativity, and holds us back from taking the risks we need to grow.

More often, we see parents trying to protect their kids from failure. They want to shield them from any discomfort or challenges, becoming 'comfort parents' thinking that this will ensure perennial happiness for their kids. But life is not going to do the same to their kids when they grow up as adults. For sure, there would be problems, issues, tensions and struggles. And, these kids who expect the world to cater to their every need would then struggle with rejection and have a hard time dealing with failure.

More so, such children often struggle with narcissism and entitlement, believing they are superior to others. This sense of entitlement can lead to further issues like anxiety, depression, and even addiction as they face the harsh realities of life. While it's natural for parents to want the best for their children, it's important to teach them resilience, the value of hard work, and the reality that life isn't always perfect.

By allowing them to experience failure and disappointment, we help them grow into grounded, empathetic individuals who understand that success is not about perfection, but about learning and evolving through life's ups and downs. For us, it's crucial to remember that failure isn't something to fear—it's a necessary part of life. We've been conditioned to chase the "perfect" image, whether it's success, happiness, or achievements, all because of the hype, surrounding these ideals. But we need to question the images and narratives we're constantly presented with.

"If you are walking through hell, keep walking", Winston Churchill.

Hardships, struggles and failures are so relevant that across cultures they were adopted and taught- either formally or informally. In ancient education systems, such as India's Gurukul, Sparta's agoge, Confucian China, and medieval European apprenticeships, hardships were central to building resilience, discipline, and wisdom. Gurukul students performed chores and practised self-control, while Spartans underwent rigorous physical training. Confucian education emphasized moral cultivation, and apprenticeships focused on developing skills and patience. Today, military academies like NDA and West Point, sports programs, and entrepreneurial education continue to expose young individuals to hardships, fostering resilience, discipline, and adaptability. Across time, these challenges shaped character and prepared individuals for life's demands.

Are we appreciating our struggles and trusting that life's imperfections, challenges and setbacks shape us?

Choose Struggle, Not Just Success

One school of thought believes that if you want something badly enough and visualize it, the universe will make it happen. But in reality, it doesn't work that way. You need to know what you want, commit to it, and most importantly, take action and work hard.

For instance- if you wish to become a pilot and fly an aircraft, you can't barely dream and visualize about it. You must also accept that it will require hard work and struggling phase. You need to choose not just the dream, but also the challenges that come with it. By doing so, not only do your chances of success increase, but you also get to know the depth and meaning. Easy money, effortless relationships, or meals without effort may seem appealing at first, but they don't bring the same fulfilment. It's the challenges we face, the hurdles we overcome, and the hard work we put in that make success truly worthwhile. When we choose to struggle, we not only learn and grow, but we also gain a deeper appreciation for the rewards that come with it.

As Albert Einstein once said, *"Struggle is the meaning of life. We are going to struggle, and that's the path to meaning."* Just like that refreshing glass of water after a long run, or the soothing bath after a tough day. Even something as simple as writing a good sentence or having a meaningful conversation. These aren't just little steps toward some bigger reward; they are the rewards. And to feel them, we have to slow down, connect with ourselves, and stop getting caught up in what we think we need to be happy.

The truth is, we're not lost. We're right here, right now. And we need to stop thinking that love or success is something that will either show up one day or never come at all. Let's embrace the life we have—flaws and all. There's nothing more powerful than someone who refuses to give up, even when everything feels tough, and instead learns to find joy in the struggle. As Brene Brown wisely said, *"Courage starts with showing up and letting ourselves be seen."*

When we stop fearing where we are and learn to be fully present, that's when the magic happens. We'll look back and realize that those challenging moments, the hard days, were actually the most beautiful part of the journey. The struggle, the growth, the pain—it's all part of learning to live fully in the present, to feel everything, and to realize just how lucky we are right now.

As Viktor Frankl beautifully put it, *"When we are no longer able to change a situation, we are challenged to change ourselves."*

Roads and Destination of Elusive Success

Success, like any innovation, isn't a single, perfect moment but a gradual process of trial and error. Failure is an inevitable part of this journey, reminding us that setbacks are universal and often lead to breakthroughs. We are never alone in facing them.

Albert Einstein struggled with early academic challenges before becoming a renowned physicist, and Walt Disney faced multiple business failures before creating the iconic Disney Empire. Oprah Winfrey was fired from her first television job, and Colonel Sanders endured numerous rejections before KFC became a global brand. Amitabh Bachchan was rejected by All India Radio for having a "voice not suitable for radio," and Dr. A.P.J. Abdul Kalam too faced many setbacks before becoming the beloved "Missile Man" and the President of India. For all of them, success must have seemed distant at first—full of rejection and failure. Yet, their persistence and belief turned their stories into examples.

"I have not failed. I've just found 10,000 ways that won't work."— Thomas A. Edison

On your journey, sometimes you may often feel success is elusive, feel like something everyone else is grabbing, but it's just not meant for you. Like a distant concept, like it's something other people are able to attain, but for some reason, it's just not in the cards for you. I am sure most of us felt this many times. Especially, in the moments when your friend passed that exam but you couldn't or your colleague got promoted but you have still been left out. Despite you feeling yourself as a strong candidate, you couldn't make it to the list. Yes, I am talking about that sense of being 'left out' that you had in those times, and out of other things, one of the most difficult was handling your – mental and emotional – well-being. What has that experience shaped you into? Have you ever calculated it?

Have you ever felt disconnected like this, or found success elusive, just out of reach? You are making plans, working hard, and putting efforts in place, but it still seems to slip away. Isn't it a strange and frustrating feeling? I can say this because I have been through this.

Undeniably, there can be a lot of reasons behind this, and it's not always about doing something wrong.

Sometimes, it's about how we approach success or what we're expecting from it.

One big reason could be setting expectations that are just too high. If you're focusing on this big, shiny idea of success without recognizing the small steps it takes to get there, it can feel like you're not making any progress, even when you really are. Another thing is comparison. With social media and success stories all around us, it's easy to feel like everyone else has it figured out while you're still struggling. But the thing is, everyone's path is different, and what you see on the outside isn't always the full picture. Next, fear of failure can also hold you back. You might feel stuck or hesitate to take risks because you're worried that things won't work out. But honestly, failure is part of the process.

Further, it could also be that you're chasing goals that don't really align with what you care about or value. If you're going after a version of success you think you "should" want, it's easy to feel disconnected from it. Timing and luck play a role too—sometimes, no matter how hard you work, the right opportunity just hasn't come along yet. That doesn't mean you're not on the right path, though. And if you're feeling burn outs or exhausted, that can make everything feel like it's further away, even if you've been putting in the work. Then, finally after many 'missed' tries, imposter syndrome can sneak in, where you feel like you don't deserve success, even when you're doing everything right.

In fact, it's a lot to deal with, but it doesn't mean you're failing. It's just part of the journey. Sometimes it takes a little patience, some self-reflection, and the willingness to keep going even when success feels far off. Have you ever felt like this, or do you think any of these things might be contributing to how you're feeling?

Self-Reflection on 'Close but Not Quite' Stances

"You do not even know how much the story you are scared to tell, could help someone else out of their isolated hell." — Jennae Cecelia.

A Near Miss with the Armed Forces- My father had always wanted my brother to join the armed forces, something that is certainly a matter of pride. However, my brother, passionate about research and science, wasn't much interested in that path. Then, one of my cousins cleared the Air Force recruitment exam. He was receiving praise and admiration from everyone around. Watching this, I felt inspired to give my father the same pride and attention. With determination, I applied for the Women Special Entry (Officers) Scheme exam and headed to the Allahabad SSB Board with my parents. After six days of rigorous testing, I was recommended by the Staff Selection Board. Out of a batch of 80, only three girls were selected, and I was one of them. That moment felt like a personal triumph—a step closer to fulfilling my father's dream.

My family celebrated my success, my classmates started calling me "lieutenant," and even distant relatives began reaching out. It seemed like I was on top of the world, with the army uniform just within reach. During the police verification process, it almost felt certain that I was going to be officially selected. But when the final list came out, my name wasn't there. Instead, it was on the waiting list, which never got cleared. I had fallen short by just one place.

An Elusive Path to Civil Services Success- A few years later, I visualized success in a different dimension—in civil services. Like an ultimate dream for many in India, where civil servants are seen as the pinnacle of honour, prestige, and respect, I too queued myself. In our society, it's almost believed that becoming a civil servant wipes away all your sins! And, the sins of your generations too! So, I decided to dive headfirst into the life of an aspirant. The first thing you're told at the onset of this journey is to abandon all worldly pleasures, live a life of salvation, and self-discipline, and stay focused. Skip family events, avoid celebrations, and forget about travelling or meeting or what so ever leisurely joy you can think of. At first, I absorbed these expectations partially, but eventually, I got fully committed to the grind. I spent three years preparing in the confines of a hostel room, and gave all my best. However, despite all my efforts, I couldn't even clear the preliminary exam in the first two attempts. I felt hopeless and decided to leave this journey.

But that was not easy either. As once you enter the life of an aspirant, it's like a maze—easy to start, but so difficult to exit. I found myself trying the same next year too. Even during pregnancy, I didn't give up, studied hard, and left no stone unturned to try my luck, now with the State Public Service Exam.

Brave enough, at eight months of pregnancy and difficult physical conditions, I appeared for the Preliminary exam—and cleared it! As I prepared for the next stage, life took a beautiful turn. I gave birth to my son, stepping into motherhood with a mix of joy and newfound responsibility. To me, this wasn't just a dream anymore; it had transformed into a goal—a mission to improve my life and circumstances. It became a way to rise above a lot of inconveniences of life. Now, with a new born in my arms, I kept studying hard. I poured myself into the second stage of it i.e. preparation for the 'Mains' exam, spending hours in the library and pausing only for the lactation breaks.

And, I did it—I cleared the Mains exam too. Bravo! I felt unstoppable, finally on the path to cracking the interview. The excitement was contagious. Everyone around was celebrating this and showering me with well-earned compliments. I was so close to the final verdict, carrying the weight of immense expectations.

When the interview day arrived, I gave it my all. A few months later, the results were announced. That misty morning, my heart sank as I scrolled through the list, unable to find my roll number. Denial consumed me—I checked the list again and again, thinking I had missed something. But the reality was unshakable; it felt like the ground had been pulled from under me. This wasn't merely a dream—it was my way to escape certain harsh realities, to expand my horizons, and to create a life worth celebrating.

Years of physical and mental effort had gone into this pursuit. For so long, I had postponed joys, thinking I'd celebrate later. Yet, that moment never came. Strangely, I didn't shed a single tear that day, but the weeks and months that followed were nothing short of horrible. I got to know from the fellow aspirants that if just one more name had made the list, it would have been mine. Rumours swirled about the exam's transparency, and people around me rallied to question its fairness. Well, some questions, though, never got answered; some only found resolution with time. The despair lingered for two to three years, and though life moved on, the ache of that chapter remains a part of me. Some failures leave marks that never fully fade, no matter how far you go beyond them.

And, Afterwards, I Was No More the Same Girl

This experience mirrors the earlier one, where success seemed so close, yet it slipped away at the last moment. I had worked hard, remained persistent, and come so far, but once again, timing, circumstances, and perhaps luck stood in my way.

Despite almost reaching the finish line, I didn't make it—missing out by a small margin. The frustration of putting in effort, gaining recognition, and still falling short left me questioning my confidence as to why I couldn't cross that final hurdle, even when everything seemed to align perfectly.

The same people who once praised my determination began calling me a "tragedy queen" and that single mark or one missed place grew far bigger than its actual value, overshadowing all my efforts.

Unfortunately, success in our society is often measured solely in economic terms or by one's status. The accumulation of wealth or social standing tends to overshadow other forms of achievement. Rarely do we pause to appreciate that gaining knowledge, broadening perspectives, or growing as a person can also be powerful markers of success.

"I think everybody should get rich and famous and do everything they ever dreamed of so they can see that it's not the answer." — *Jim Carrey*

Well, after shedding endless tears, narrating my "failure stories", shouting in closed rooms, and lying empty stomach on my bed for days, I came to a painful realization that I had everything—except happiness. I had tied my joy entirely to the yardstick of success, forgetting that success can be found in small wins, and sometimes, it just needs to be rerouted. Looking back, I realize I shouldn't have put all my hopes and efforts into one single goal. I had motherhood to celebrate—a profound achievement that brought joy and purpose into my life. My journey as an aspirant wasn't wasted either; it expanded my knowledge base, sharpened my skills, and even led me to earn another postgraduate degree.

"Life is so damned hard, so damned hard... It just hurts people and hurts people, until it finally hurts them so that they can't be hurt ever any more. That's the last and worst thing it does."

— F. Scott Fitzgerald

I was no longer the amateur who had first stepped into this challenging path. The experience transformed me, giving me a deeper understanding of the world and my own capabilities. This exam wasn't the 'finish line' of my life—it was just one chapter. I needed to uncover the other potentials within me, to embrace the opportunities waiting beyond that one goal. Success isn't always about reaching the summit; sometimes, it's also about finding new peaks to climb.

Equally important, I shouldn't have felt that I was answerable to anyone for not meeting societal expectations. No one among them had walked the path I did—the life of minimalism, surviving with the least, and dedicating months and years to a single library chair. No time for myself, all duty-bound, following my routine religiously.

People who made generalised statements were barely sitting in their everyday comfort and had perhaps never understood the labour. And, experienced the pain of those emotional highs and lows—the moments of feeling utterly defeated and the moments of belief that I could conquer it all. I carried each emotion, every flicker of doubt and hope, and pushed forward with unwavering determination. The truth is, the only person I owed answers to is myself. It was my journey, my struggle, and my growth. I fought battles no one saw, overcame hurdles no one understood, and emerged stronger with them. This was my story, and I was the only one who could truly judge it.

Henceforth, my idea of success became detached from external validations, approvals, and expectations. I began focusing on my own growth, peace, and satisfaction. I realized that success isn't about meeting societal standards or living up to someone else's definition—it's about staying true to yourself, learning from your experiences, and embracing the journey. The only measure of success that truly matters is how content and fulfilled I feel within myself.

"Success is not the key to happiness, Happiness is the key to success".

I stopped measuring myself by a constant yardstick of success. I realized that happiness and sadness are habits we can choose to cultivate or break. Over trivial issues, I asked myself—what do I choose? I decided not to give undue importance to either. I understood that nothing lasts forever, not even the toughest mental state. Change might not come immediately, but it comes eventually. All I needed was to trust the process, stay resilient, and embrace the present without letting external outcomes define my worth.

"When we celebrate life, we embrace creativity, whether it's through music, art, or shared laughter. Celebrations are magnets because they offer a chance to bond, to share in the joy, and to create experiences that remind us of the love and connection we have with others."

I began seeking success and happiness in new-found dimensions—through expressing myself, writing, and storytelling. Whether in classrooms or on canvas, I discovered a deeper sense of fulfilment. It wasn't about external recognition anymore; it was about tapping into my creativity, sharing my voice, and connecting with others through words and art. These outlets allowed me to rediscover my passions and embrace the beauty of personal expression.

More so, I started counting each small win, each recognition, and every step up the ladder as a contribution. I stopped crying over my failures; instead, they became stepping stones to explore versatility and endurance within myself. In those moments, I realized that true success lies in following what makes me feel alive, not in chasing society's definition of achievement.

And, this is going to stay with me for the most of my life. People's expectations don't trouble me anymore. Failures don't shake me as much. I know things can take turns in unexpected and un-assumed ways too. I have learned to live in harmony with these facts, and self-propelling me now, setting my own standards, and working toward them. A few I achieve, and a few I still don't. But at least, I try. What I can simply say now is— I have better stories to tell!

Success isn't always linear. Also, isn't always about the final result, but also about the lessons learned and the person we become through the process. Despite our best efforts, things didn't always unfold as planned, and that wasn't a reflection of our worth or capabilities. This realization made us more adaptable, finding strength in moments of uncertainty, reframing goals, and moving forward.

In the end, success isn't rejecting me—it's redefining itself for me. It doesn't come to those who shy away from struggle, who remain broken without the will to heal, or who rely solely on others to shape their path. Success demands inner strength, resilience, and self-reliance. It doesn't align with an outer locus of control or the irrelevant yardsticks society imposes. It doesn't lie in a hollow sense of achievement, nor is it about endlessly wanting more or fixating on a distant destination. Instead, success asks us to create our own definitions, rooted in struggle, failure, and authenticity. It's not something to be acquired—it's something to be lived. It's not a prize waiting at the finish line but a reflection of how I rise, persist, and evolve in the face of life's challenges. When I stop seeking it in all the wrong places and start embracing the journey, I'll realize that success was never truly elusive—it was simply waiting for me to become the person worthy of it.

CHAPTER 8
MINIMALISM AND MARKETING OF EMOTIONS

Chapter 8
Minimalism and Marketing of Emotions

Since the day we are born, the world seems to whisper—or rather shout—that we need more. More toys as children, more achievements as students, more possessions as adults. Advertisements constantly bombard us with the same message: "More is always better." But is it really? The truth is, these promises often ring hollow. Driven by the marketing of emotions, consumerism convinces us that happiness lies in the next purchase, the next upgrade, the next 'more.' Yet, while chasing this illusion, we risk losing sight of what truly matters —our peace, our purpose, and the simple joys that make life meaningful.

Like guiding beacons of life, I found calm in minimalism and simplicity. Minimalism is an art of 'living with less' but finding more—more peace, more clarity, and more purpose. In a world full of noise and excess, it reminds me to strip away the unnecessary, and create space for purpose, peace, and genuine connection. And, focus on what truly matters and let go of what doesn't. To me, minimalism and simplicity are more than just lifestyle choices—it's a profound sense of clarity that has been with me for as long as I can remember. It's not just a concept I picked up along the way; it's deeply rooted in my upbringing. My mother, who always advocated for possessing less, consuming less, wasting less, and working hard, taught me to embrace simplicity from a young age.

I was brought up in a rural setting within a producer's family—a farmer's family in a village where we were more of producers than consumers. Most of the everyday things, including food grains, milk products, and vegetables, were all grown on farms, and we hardly had to buy much of these things. Moreover, as a part of the community culture, I saw consumerism as largely discouraged. I remember instances when someone needed any of these items in bulk, say milk or vegetables, and other members of the society would reach out to them, offering their own share to help mitigate the need. This way, there was hardly any reason to rely on buying.

Back then, minimalism wasn't a trendy buzzword or a lifestyle movement—it was just how we lived. Well, as a Management Graduate, I understand that consuming less may not be good for an economy but for a community, it was certainly good. For, it fostered sustainable co-existence and a balance—between consumption and preservation, between personal needs and the well-being of the environment. And, for me, it's a way of life to anchor and empower me for most of the times in life.

After completing my Bachelor's in Science, I moved to a metro city to pursue an MBA and saw that the world around me hummed a different tune. Consumerism—the pursuit of more—was everywhere. The advertisements, the social cues, and the promises of happiness through acquisition. It was all so loud, so pervasive, and so persuasive. I studied the intricate mechanics of consumerism, dissecting its strategies and its grip on human emotions. Meanwhile, I learned how brands tapped into our desires, our fears, and even our insecurities to sell us not just products but ideas of who we should be. The art of emotional marketing was fascinating and, at times, unsettling.

This made me wonder how powerful the marketing of emotions could be, how it could make us yearn for things we didn't need, and how it stood in stark contrast to the minimalist philosophy I held close. This realization wasn't just academic; it was personal. It made me question how often we let external influences dictate our choices, and how often we trade simplicity for the illusion of fulfilment. This chapter is a journey through those realizations—an exploration of how minimalism and the marketing of emotions intersect, the lessons we can draw from both, and how we can reclaim our sense of balance in a world that often equates worth with consumption.

The Power of 'Less'

How often have you heard someone say, "I just want a simpler life"? It's a sentiment that resonates with many in today's fast-paced and cluttered world. People often long for a life with fewer distractions, less mayhem, and more clarity.

Having less is quite powerful. Living with less isn't about deprivation rather, it allows you to exercise more-more control of your finances, time, energy and hence, life. The power of subtraction is transformative. Minimalism has a proven positive impact on mental and emotional well-being. When you let go of what's unnecessary, whether its physical clutter, an overbooked schedule, or mental distractions, you create room for peace and purpose. For me, minimalism is more than decluttering a closet or tidying up a room. It's about creating clarity in my mind and peace in my heart. When I let go of things I don't need—whether it's physical stuff, unnecessary commitments, or even unhelpful thoughts—I feel lighter, freer, and more in control of my life.

"Minimalism is the mind-set, and simplicity is the outcome".

Minimalism, as a lifestyle and mind-set, has gained considerable traction in recent years. Originating from the art and design world, minimalism advocates for simplicity and intentionality in both physical and mental arenas.

Simplicity is visually exciting and also fun to deal with. It saves cognitive resources and empowers you with autonomy, mental space, and greater self-awareness. It enhances competence, helps foster better sleep, and allows people to prioritize what truly enriches their lives. Research supports this- people in organized and simple environments are less likely to feel stressed or anxious and more likely to experience better moods, increased energy, and emotional balance.

Simplicity is attractive.

Simplicity is calming.

Simplicity inspires creativity.

Simplicity allows balance.

Simplicity reduces confusion.

Simplicity allows space to breathe.

Ultimately, minimalism isn't just about having less—it's about creating space for more. More meaning, more joy, and more intentional living. If you've ever longed for a simpler life, start by asking yourself, *"What can I let go of today?"* Often, the answer lies in subtraction, opening the door to clarity, fulfilment, and balance.

Minimalism offers threefold benefits- physically, psychologically, and socially. Physically, it creates organized, serene spaces that reduce stress and enhance productivity. Psychologically, it promotes mindfulness and clarity, easing anxiety and encouraging intentional choices. Socially, it deepens connections by focusing on quality over quantity in relationships. Further, three core principles of minimalism -practising intentionality, decluttering emotional baggage, and prioritizing experiences over possessions – serve like pillars.

Intentionality is about focusing on what truly matters by deliberately keeping what adds value and letting go of what doesn't. It's about prioritizing activities, commitments, and relationships that bring joy and meaning to your life.

Decluttering emotional baggage is a lot like tidying up a messy room. Just as piles of clutter can make a space feel overwhelming, unresolved emotions like past grievances, unresolved conflicts, or self-doubt can weigh heavily on your heart and mind. When we take the time to reflect, forgive, and let go, we make space for healthier, more honest, and meaningful connections. Sometimes, it's as simple as a heartfelt conversation, and other times, seeking support can help—but the result is always worth it.

Prioritizing Experiences over Possession encourages us to focus on creating moments and memories rather than collecting material things. In relationships, it can deeply enhance connections by prioritizing shared experiences like travelling, dining together, or simply spending quality time. These moments not only build meaningful memories but also enrich relationships, fostering closeness and mutual appreciation.

By embracing these principles, minimalism becomes a powerful tool to enrich your life and relationships.

Simple Living Philosophies across Cultures

The concept of minimalism may appear anti-business, and anti-consumerist. Strongly in contrast to overconsumption, Minimalism focuses on what is essential. It de-clutters the unnecessary and insists on living a life of purpose. As a philosophy and lifestyle, it has deep connections to almost all ancient cultures and aligns with spiritual and cultural practices that date back thousands of years. Around the world, various practices and traditions have reflected the core tenets of minimalism—simplicity, essentialism, and intentional living.

In India, minimalism is deeply intertwined with spiritual traditions. Practices such as sannyasa (renunciation) and yoga encourage individuals to shed material possessions and desires to focus on spiritual growth. Sannyasa (Renunciation) in Hindu and Jain traditions emphasize detachment from materialism. Sannyasis, those who renounce worldly life, live simply, often owning little more than basic clothing and a few necessities. Yoga and Aparigraha practices, especially through the Yamas and Niyamas (ethical guidelines), encourage simplicity and non-attachment. Aparigraha, one of the Yamas, promotes non-possession and contentment with what one has. The lifestyle of ascetics and monks in India, who live in solitary spaces with minimal possessions, focusing solely on meditation, is a direct reflection of minimalism.

In Japan, minimalism is deeply embedded in Zen Buddhism and the concept of wabi-sabi. Zen teaches the importance of simplicity, mindfulness, and non-attachment to material goods. The minimalist Japanese aesthetic emphasizes functionality and the beauty of imperfection. Wabi-sabi is the appreciation of things that are simple, rustic, and impermanent, such as the unevenness of a handmade tea cup. The minimalist design of traditional Japanese homes, with clean lines, natural materials, and a focus on space, is an expression of this philosophy. The Japanese tea ceremony (Chadō) is an embodiment of minimalism. Every aspect—from the tea utensils to the space in which the ceremony occurs—is designed to create a simple, serene experience that focuses on the present moment.

Scandinavian cultures, particularly Denmark and Sweden, embrace minimalist concepts through the concepts of hygge and lagom. While hygge is often associated with coziness, it also promotes a minimalist approach to living—valuing comfort over excess. It emphasizes creating peaceful and meaningful moments with loved ones, in simple, pleasant environments. Lagom means "not too little, not too much, just right." It encourages balance and contentment, rejecting overconsumption and promoting a lifestyle where everything is moderate. It aligns with minimalism by emphasizing only keeping what is necessary and enjoyable, both in the home and in personal practices. In Sweden, you'll find small, well-designed apartments that focus on functionality with as little excess as possible. Lagom encourages buying only what is truly needed and valued.

Buddhist teachings also emphasize moderation—avoiding extremes of indulgence or asceticism. The Middle Path, as taught by the Buddha, encourages balance and simplicity. Buddhist monks across Asia often live in monasteries with minimal possessions, focusing on meditation, prayer, and simplicity. Native American, African, and Aboriginal Australian cultures, have long practised minimalist living in harmony with nature. These cultures emphasize sustainable living, valuing the land and its resources, and ensuring sustainability for future generations. This kind of environmental minimalism reflects a philosophy of living in balance with the Earth.

In the U.S., the minimalism movement began in the mid-20th century, right after World War II. With the economy booming and mass production on the rise, there was an explosion of material goods. People were constantly bombarded with ads and the pressure to buy more. This led to a feeling of being overwhelmed by too many possessions and the need to always acquire more. The minimalist movement in art and lifestyle grew as a response to all this excess.

Following it, in the 2000s, minimalism as a lifestyle really took off. People started to feel disconnected from materialism and wanted a simpler life. Influencers like

Joshua Fields Millburn and Ryan Nicodemus (The Minimalists) helped spread the message through their blog, documentaries, and books. They encouraged people to declutter, focus on what really mattered, and live with fewer possessions. The idea was to reduce stress, find more purpose, and focus on experiences instead of things. Many people across the U.S. started downsizing, even living in tiny houses, to clear out the clutter and prioritize what truly brought them happiness and fulfilment.

Minimalism is neither a new trend nor out of fashion. A few brands, such as Marie Kondo's Tidying Up or companies like Muji, are using minimalist principles in their marketing by highlighting simplicity, quality, and utility. Also, eco-friendly brands like Patagonia promote the idea of buying less but choosing better-quality, longer-lasting items, resonating with consumers who value thoughtful consumption. These campaigns appeal to consumers' emotions around peace, clarity, and intentional living, aligning with minimalist values. Adopting minimalism can lead to a more intentional, fulfilling life as it enables individuals to prioritize what truly matters in life—whether that's experiences, relationships, or personal well-being and fosters peace in a cluttered world.

Emotional Pull vs. Minimalist Calm

Have you ever bought something you didn't need, just because you were strongly influenced by an advertisement or a marketer? And then regretted it afterwards, never using the product or using it just once or twice? I'm sure we all have that one dress, shoe, tie, or bag we bought just because we were searching for a positive emotion. Do you know why that happened? Because the marketer made you feel inadequate, as if you needed the product to feel better. They tapped into your desire to feel great, positive, or cherished, and you made the purchase in a rush, thinking that your search for "feeling great" would end there. But soon, you felt low again and fell into the same trap. And, interestingly this marketing trap works for all of us.

Minimalism and marketing of emotions often collide because marketing taps into our emotions to make us feel like we need more, while minimalism teaches us to focus on what truly matters. While ads may stir feelings of wanting more, minimalism encourages us to find contentment in less, challenging the constant push to consume.

In the world of 'surround sound marketing'—a tactic to reach consumers in every way possible—we're constantly surrounded by media, billboards, hoardings, digital screens, pop-ups, and more. Every fraction of a second, we're triggered by marketing efforts from businesses. This constant bombardment of images, sounds, and sensations overloads our brains with information, making it hard to process everything at once, leading to poor decision-making. In this digital age, we're constantly bombarded with information, images, videos, and pop-ups. It's hard to even find yourself amidst all this noise. Did you know that on average, a person encounters 4,000 to 10,000 ads every single day? From billboards and TV commercials to social media pop-ups and website banners, advertising is everywhere. More so, the rise of digital platforms like social media, search engines, and streaming services has dramatically increased how often we're exposed to marketing messages. No wonder it feels like we're constantly being sold something!

So, what exactly are they selling us? Hopes? Dreams? Happiness? Satisfaction? Positivity? Creativity? Calmness? Love? Or just their products—through the marketing of emotions? In contrast to the idea of minimalism, aren't we becoming hedonists, wanting more and more, triggered by the feeling of having less and less?

Studies show that emotions play a huge role in our purchasing decisions. Consumers would often make choices based on emotions, personal feelings, and connections, rather than on facts, features, or experiences. Did you know that 95% of our buying decisions are driven by our subconscious mind? Emotions guide us first, and then we come up with logical reasons to justify them afterwards. For example, you might buy a pair of sneakers because they make you feel confident or trendy, and later tell yourself it's because they're durable or on sale.

Marketers know this well. Research proves it. Marketing campaigns based on emotional content perform significantly better than those based on rational content—31% better, compared to just 16% for rational ads. Think about an ad that made you laugh, tear up, or feel nostalgic—it stays with you longer than a simple, fact-based ad. For instance, a heart-warming commercial showing a child saving up to buy a meaningful gift for a parent may not directly sell a product, but it creates a strong emotional bond with the brand. That emotional connection can nudge you toward choosing that brand the next time you see it.

Consider the iconic Budweiser Super Bowl ads featuring adorable puppies and majestic horses. These commercials do not directly showcase the product itself but tap into emotions like loyalty, companionship, and love. The result? Consumers feel a warm connection to the brand, translating to increased loyalty and purchase intent. These ads highlight how emotional storytelling can create a memorable experience, making it less about the product and more about the feel. Check a few here–

Navigating Emotional Triggers

The impact of emotional marketing on consumer behaviour is undeniable, and I'm sure we've all felt it. As someone who has lived with minimalism as a guiding principle, I can't help but notice the contrast between the emotional triggers used by brands and the way minimalism teaches us to live intentionally. Let's break it down.

Happiness: Think about Coca-Cola's "Share a Coke" campaign, for instance. I'm sure you've experienced the joy of finding a bottle with your name on it, or a loved one's name, and how it made the simple act of drinking a Coke feel special. It's all about creating a connection, right? The campaign didn't just sell a drink—it sold the idea of joy, nostalgia, and personal connection.

Similarly, Cadbury's ads often associate their chocolate with moments of celebration and happiness, tying the product to emotional milestones. Tesla, with its promise of a sustainable future, promotes hope and positivity. While these campaigns tap into our emotions, they also push us toward more consumption. But here's where minimalism changes the game. It asks us to question whether we need to buy more to feel happy, or if we can find contentment in the simpler and essential things around us.

Guilt: Then there's guilt—another powerful emotion marketers know how to exploit. Non-profits often use guilt to spur donations, with heart-wrenching images of suffering children or messages like "Just ₹10 can save a life." It makes you feel like you must act, right now. Similarly, luxury brands and personal care companies use guilt to make us feel inadequate. Think about how many ads for skincare or weight loss products make you feel like you're not doing enough to care for yourself.

The underlying message is that we need to buy these products to be better versions of ourselves. I've often found myself reflecting on how marketers have made me feel guilty for not having this or that. But minimalism challenges that narrative. It's about rejecting the notion that we're incomplete without more, and instead focusing on what we truly need. For me, it's been freeing to realize that I don't need to buy into that guilt-driven marketing to feel good about myself or my life.

Anger: Anger, too, is used in advertising to provoke strong reactions. Take Nike's controversial ad featuring Colin Kaepernick. It sparked heated debates on racial inequality and police brutality, resonating deeply with people who care about social justice. Similarly, Always'#LikeAGirl campaign challenged gender stereotypes, using anger to empower people to rethink the phrase and its negative connotations.

Anger can create urgency—making us feel like we need to act, to fight against injustice, or to stand for something. I can see how these emotional appeals can drive action, but as someone who values minimalism, I also wonder if this constant push to act on every emotional trigger is sustainable. Are we meant to buy into everything because we're emotionally pushed toward it, or can we make more mindful, intentional choices? Minimalism, for me, encourages me to step back and decide what's truly important, rather than being swept up in every emotional cause that comes my way.

Fear: Then there's fear, one of the most effective tools in marketing. Brands like Norton and McAfee use fear of hacking and identity theft to sell their security software. Campaigns warning about the dangers of not saving enough for retirement or the risks of an unhealthy lifestyle all prey on our fears.

But here's the thing—minimalism teaches us to confront our fears, to simplify our lives, and to focus on what we truly need. Instead of fearing what might go wrong, it's about being intentional in our choices and reducing unnecessary worries. For me, embracing minimalism has helped me manage my fears, whether it's the fear of not having enough or the fear of making the wrong decision. By simplifying, I've learned to reduce the noise.

Dealing with Emotional Traps

Emotions are the invisible threads that connect us to the world, making every experience richer and more meaningful. They shape our decisions, fuel our dreams, and remind us that it's okay to stumble. For example, the quiet pride of watching a child take their first steps or the rush of anger when someone cuts you off in traffic—these moments may seem small, but they define how we relate to the world. Being human isn't about perfection; it's about feeling, healing, and growing through the highs and lows.

In this age of constant advertising, it's easy to get caught up in emotional marketing. But by recognizing these tactics and focusing on your own priorities, you can regain control. Whether it's FOMO from flash sales or the aspirational lifestyles depicted in ads, awareness helps you step back and evaluate your true needs. Emotional triggers like love, fear, happiness, and nostalgia often push us to make impulsive purchases or chase idealized lifestyles. As humans, we're naturally wired to respond to emotions, and marketers leverage this to nudge us toward purchases. They craft stories that make products feel personal—whether it's overcoming hardship, celebrating love, or achieving success. Ads that tie material goods to feelings of love, success, or self-worth can make us believe our happiness is tied to what we own. And campaigns that romanticize family or career success can set unattainable expectations, leading to stress, anxiety, or feelings of failure. These stories bypass our logic and make us act on emotion instead of practicality. Breaking free requires us to have mindfulness; pausing before a purchase, and asking if it's something we truly need or just an emotional impulse. Recognizing these tactics empowers us to make decisions that truly add value to our lives. For instance, when you see an ad for a fitness gadget promising life-changing results, pause and ask yourself- Do I really need this? Or am I just being emotionally influenced? The more mindful we are, the better we can make decisions that align with what we truly need, not fleeting desires.

Falling into emotional marketing traps happens to all of us, often without realizing it. Marketers understand how emotions drive decisions, using psychological triggers and social pressures to make us act on feelings rather than logic. Over time, this can create dissatisfaction, as we realize the products we buy don't deliver the emotional fulfilment promised. It can also lead to financial strain and emotional emptiness, reinforcing unrealistic standards and offering superficial solutions to deeper personal needs.

We've Come A Full Circle

When I think about how we've moved from simpler times to today's consumer-driven world, it's pretty eye-opening. Over the years, our relationship with possessions has shifted dramatically, from ancient civilizations that valued simplicity to a modern world of excess. Let's take a quick look at how our views on consumerism and minimalism have evolved.

Ancient Times: People lived simply, focusing on basic needs like food, shelter, and survival. Philosophers like Socrates and Aristotle believed happiness wasn't about having more things but about cultivating virtue and knowledge. In cultures like India and China, spiritual teachings like Buddhism and Taoism emphasized living with less to grow spiritually—a lesson we could still learn from today.

Medieval Times: Life was largely influenced by religion and feudal systems, where simplicity and humility were virtues. The church taught that owning too much distracted from spiritual growth. Most people didn't have the means for excess, and simplicity was often a necessity, not a choice.

Renaissance and Enlightenment: Individualism and self-expression took centre stage, and people began accumulating things not just for survival but as symbols of wealth and personal taste. Yet, thinkers like Rousseau warned that chasing material wealth could lead to dissatisfaction—a conflict that has only grown over time.

Industrial Revolution: Mass production made goods cheaper and more accessible, and consumerism really took off. It became about more than survival; it was about showing off prosperity, and "more" became the goal. Ads started convincing us we needed things we didn't even know existed.

20th Century: After World War II, mass production, advertising, and TV shaped our relationship with possessions. "Keeping up with the Joneses" became the cultural norm, and consumerism dominated, leading many to chase the wrong things—more possessions, bigger houses, and the latest gadgets.

21st Century: Now, we're starting to see a shift back to simplicity. Movements like minimalism are gaining momentum as people realize that owning more doesn't bring happiness. Instead, living intentionally and focusing on what truly matters—relationships, experiences, and peace of mind—has become the new goal. Sustainability and conscious living are on the rise, and it feels like we're rediscovering the wisdom of the past while embracing the benefits of modern life.

Finding Balance

The difference between emotional marketing or consumerism and minimalism is pretty straightforward. Marketing often taps into our emotions, making us feel rushed, inadequate, or even scared, just to push us to buy more. Minimalism, however, encourages us to slow down, question those feelings, and focus on what truly matters. It's about making intentional choices that align with our values, not chasing after every new trend. For me, embracing minimalism has brought more meaning to my life by cutting out the emotional manipulation that comes with advertising.

Minimalism isn't just about buying less—it's also about creating a sustainable future. By reducing unnecessary purchases, we conserve resources, reduce waste, and live more consciously. It teaches us to manage our finances better, focusing on what we truly need, saving for the future, and not getting swept up in the latest trends. For future generations, learning to manage money in this way is essential. It helps break the cycle of consumerism and leads to more fulfilling lives, with a healthy financial mind-set and intentional choices.

Moreover, as we look back on the evolution of consumerism and minimalism, it's clear that we've come full circle. From ancient simplicity to modern excess, and now back to a place where we're starting to appreciate less, there's a beautiful balance to be found. We're not rejecting the conveniences and luxuries of modern life; instead, we're learning how to live more intentionally, choosing quality over quantity, and focusing on what truly makes us happy.

We see both emotional marketing and minimalism tap into our emotions, but in very different ways. While marketing uses emotions like happiness, guilt, or fear to drive us to buy things we may not need, minimalism invites us to embrace simplicity, make intentional choices, and focus on what truly brings us joy and purpose. For me, it's been a journey of letting go of what doesn't serve me, and in doing so, I've found a deeper connection to myself and the world around me.

Well, it's an ongoing journey of self-evolution, but I believe it's one that's worth taking. Because, in the end, living with less can truly give us so much more.

CHAPTER 9
THE UNEXPLORED DARK UNIVERSE INSIDE

Chapter 9
The Unexplored Dark Universe Inside

Who Am I?

My life? It's hard to explain. It hasn't been a thrilling adventure like I once dreamed, but it hasn't been dull either. It's been steady—ups, downs, and moments of quiet growth. I've been lucky, and I know that not everyone can say the same.

But let me tell you this—I am not special. I'm just a person with ordinary thoughts, living an ordinary life. There won't be statues in my name, and someday, my story will be forgotten. But I've loved deeply, with everything I have, and for me, that has always been enough.

The romantics might call my life a love story; cynics might see it as bittersweet or a fighter's story. For me, it's both. I've had struggles, but I've always chosen the path that I felt right. And even with all the bumps along the way, I wouldn't change much of the things. As time passes, the journey feels harder. The road is still there, but it's littered with life's challenges. Even so, I keep moving forward.

I don't need guarantees—I live for possibilities. Call me a dreamer or a fool, but I believe that miracles, no matter how unlikely, do happen in real life. So, every day, I hold on to hope, to love, and to the belief that life still has something extraordinary in store for me.

"Neither this is true, nor is that. The truth is you—the one who sees both."

Who am I? I often find it hard to answer this question. When I try to explain, it feels like something always gets in the way—my values, my standards, and even the way I see myself. I end up sharing only parts of who I am, leaving out the rest, which makes me feel like I'm not giving a full picture.

Many times, I feel strange to process phrases like "I'm really honest," or "I'm not easy to get along with," or even, "I'm good at reading other people's emotions." But I've also seen that people contradict themselves. The ones who say they're honest sometimes make excuses to get what they want, and the ones who claim to understand others' feelings can fall for flattery. So, it makes me wonder—how well do we really know ourselves?

The more I think about it, the more I realize that the personalities we usually identify ourselves with is a collection of fixed emotional images. We may take on different roles in life—mother, father, lover, student, teacher, worker or fighter—but none of these roles define us completely. They are temporary, passing through us, and we step into them as the situation requires.

We're all kind of like multi-personalities, aren't we? We shift and adapt to whatever role we need to play at the moment. One minute, we're focused, determined, and driven, and the next, we can drop that persona and move on to something else, just like that. It's almost like we have this superpower inside us that let us becoming what we need to be in any given moment, and then just as easily unbecoming what doesn't fit anymore. It's crazy how much potential our brains have, often beyond what we can even imagine. Scientists have proven it too—our brains have this crazy capacity that goes way beyond what we typically think they can do.

Like many of us, I'm on a journey to find myself—not through the eyes of others, but through my own. Some may focus on my strengths, while others will point out only flaws. The truth is, I am both. I am a blend of the things I've done and haven't done, shaped by the people I've met, the situations I've faced, and the circumstances I've experienced. Every part of me, good and bad, contributes to who I am.

And the thing is, we all have a dark, hidden, unknown—untapped and unexplored universe inside us. We might not even realize it's there, but it's this whole hidden space. Just like dark matter, and dark energy exist in the fundamentals of physics, a part of us remains mysterious, unseen, and yet deeply influential. Dark matter, though invisible, shapes the structure of the universe through its gravitational effects. Similarly, there are aspects of us—hidden thoughts, emotions, and parts of our identity—that influence who we are, even if we can't always see or understand them. Dark energy, which accelerates the expansion of the universe, mirrors the unseen forces within us—motivations, drives, and desires—that push us forward in ways we might not fully grasp.

Both dark matter and dark energy remain largely unknown, yet their presence is felt in profound ways. Similarly, the untapped parts of ourselves may guide our paths, even when we don't fully comprehend their influence. It's all there, just waiting for us to discover it.

The Unseen Us

It's fascinating when you think about how much our brains are capable of. We often limit ourselves by thinking we can only do so much, but in reality, our brains are capable of far more than we realize. Research has shown that the human brain is incredibly adaptable and powerful. Neuroscientist Dr. Norman Doidge in his book *The Brain That Changes Itself* talks about neuroplasticity—the brain's ability to rewire itself in response to experiences, learning, or injury. This ability means that our brains can constantly change, grow, and develop, which suggests we're capable of far more than we give ourselves credit for.

What's even more intriguing is how, in certain situations, we tap into parts of our brain that we don't usually use. Studies have found that when people are placed in life-threatening situations, they sometimes access a kind of hyper-focus, achieving things they never thought possible. Athletes, for example, are often able to perform extraordinary feats under pressure—like a runner finishing a marathon in record time, or a person lifting an enormous weight they've never been able to lift before—showing how much—untapped potential we have. Our brains are like a vast, unexplored universe, with untapped potential waiting to be discovered, and all it takes is the right circumstances, mind-set, or focus to unlock it.

Still Here, Still Exploring

"Yes, I want to teach and learn too. Both, because I've had life-changing experiences that need to be shared and learnt from because there's always more to understand, more perspectives to explore, and more ways to grow."

I once came across a list called "The 10 Most Painful Events in Life." As I read through it, I remembered going through many of them—losing loved ones, dealing with broken relationships, facing career setbacks, and struggling with feelings of failure. Each one felt impossible to get through at the time, like everything I thought was stable was being torn apart. I remembered nights spent in silence, my thoughts feeling too heavy to carry, and mornings that greeted me with a dull ache, like the world had forgotten to bring the light. The pain felt slow and never-ending, and no amount of motivation could fix it. I promised myself I wouldn't end my life today. I'd tell myself, "I'm still here. I don't know what comes next, but I have to keep going."

"It's you who's stuck with me, little warrior. Not letting' you go now."

"I want to see my story unfold," I told myself. I had heard that after every low, there's a high. I wondered if it would be my turn. I had read that time always turns around—would it happen for me? They say hard work and patience pay off—would that be true for me too? When sleep feels impossible, calm your mind by dreaming of the adventures ahead and the journey you've already taken. Wrap your arms around yourself, and as you hold yourself, remind yourself of this, "I've got you."

But I won't say I immediately got up and started working on myself. No, that didn't happen right away. Pain has a way of numbing you, and deeper pain makes you even more-numb. Everyone responds to pain differently—some bounce back quickly, and others take years. But with every struggle, something quiet inside me grew stronger. Time comes, when life also nudges you to look out the window and see the sunshine, feel the breeze, and trust the process.

No matter, how badly the forest was burned by fire, new trees will still grow with the rain. The forest will be lush again. This thought helped remind me of my own strength and how suffering can lead to growth. What stood out most was how everyone faces their own struggles, and though they're personal. However, in some way, we all have things in common- in joys and in sufferings- both. Life tests all of us and check your patience, your endurance, and your ability to keep going.

"If you asked most people if they believe in love, they'd probably say no. But that's not really how they feel— it's just their way of protecting themselves from wanting it. They do believe in love, but act like they don't until it's safe. Most people would let go of this denial thought if they had the chance, though many never get that opportunity."

Each loss, and each challenge has changed how I see things. It's taught me to appreciate the small things— the kindness of others, moments of peace, and just the strength it takes to keep going. Now, when I think about that list of 'painful events of life', it's not just a reminder of the pain I went through. It's a reminder of the strength I've gained and the life I've rebuilt, little by little. In the darkest times, I found something powerful—a small spark of hope deep inside me, telling me to keep going. It said, "There's more ahead." That spark grew stronger as I started to notice the small, healing things around me—a soothing conversation with parents, comfortable handholding, the beauty of a sunrise, the simple act of breathing through the pain, and of course the rewards of 'writing'. Slowly, I realized that life, even though full of challenges, also has moments of grace waiting to be found.

Each painful experience became a part of my story—not something that defines me, but something that teaches me how to rise, heal, and keep moving forward. That realization turned my pain into purpose. It reminded me that while I can't control what happens to me, I can control how I respond. And in that response, I found my strength. The process of rebuilding became my greatest lesson.

One Step at a Time

Often, we find ourselves startled by life's curveballs. Whether it's a job shake-up, a relationship shift, or even a personal realization that takes us by surprise, these moments remind us how easy it is to assume things will stay the same. But here's the thing—those little surprises usually reveal something valuable—maybe a new opportunity, a lesson we needed, or even just a reminder to stay flexible. Adapting to unexpected change isn't always easy, but there are ways to make it less jarring.

Elisabeth Kübler-Ross (1926–2004), a Swiss-American psychiatrist renowned for her ground-breaking work on death, dying, and grief, introduced the "Five Stages of Grief" model—Denial, Anger, Bargaining, Depression, and Acceptance—in her seminal book *On Death and Dying* (1969). This model, initially developed to describe the emotional stages terminally ill patients experience, has since been widely applied to various forms of loss, including bereavement, divorce, and other life transitions. Her work remains a cornerstone in the fields of psychology, palliative care, and grief counselling. These stages don't necessarily follow a linear path and can overlap.

Denial – It begins with Denial, as the mind's initial response to overwhelming pain, shielding us from the full impact of loss. When I lost my brother, in havoc, I first refused to believe that. The short-lived denial phase was a way of holding onto hope, a fragile defence against the rawness of reality.

Anger – Then comes anger. When denial faded, anger took its place—a fiery reaction to the hurt and helplessness I felt. I was mad at life for being so unfair, and even at myself for not doing more. "Why did this happen? Why didn't I see it coming?" These questions haunted me. Anger is isolating, yet it felt powerful, like a way to assert control over a situation that had spun out of my grasp. Even though it was painful, expressing this anger became a step toward processing my grief.

Bargaining - Bargaining brought a desperate desire to undo the loss. We bargain with God, or people or if possible with every little thing around, in all our capacities. I found myself thinking, "If only this had been there differently," or "What if I'd been more attentive, would things have been different?" I even prayed or made promises to the universe, hoping it would somehow bring him back. Through bargaining, I was postponing acceptance, trying to rewrite the past to avoid facing the finality of the loss.

"Getting over it? The words feel hollow. Recovering from a minor wound is one thing; losing someone you love is another. The pain may soften over time, and I may learn to live with it, but life will never be the same. Every moment is a reminder—his absence reshapes everything I do. Simple joys, shared memories, and even daily routines feel different now. I'm learning to navigate this loss, but I know I'll never be whole again. A part of me is gone with him, and I'll carry that ache forever."

Depression - When it became clear that nothing would change, a deep sadness set in. Days blended into nights as I withdrew from friends and activities. It felt as though a weight had settled on my chest, making it hard to breathe or find joy in anything. I cried at the smallest triggers—a song we loved, a relevant movie scene, a favourite place we visited. Each day, I woke up expecting to see him or hear his voice. I clung to routine, avoiding places that reminded me of him and convincing myself that they would walk through the door any moment. Depression wasn't just about missing them; it was about facing the void that his absence had left in our lives.

Acceptance - Acceptance didn't come in a sudden moment of clarity—it arrived in small, gradual steps. It took longer and longer time, even years too, when we began to cherish the good memories without being overwhelmed by them. I learned to live with the pain, not in spite of it, but alongside it. Acceptance didn't mean forgetting or erasing the loss but understanding that life could go on. It was in moments like being with friends again or rediscovering my passions that I realized healing was possible. Acceptance wasn't the end of grief but a new beginning, one that allowed me to honour the past while embracing the future.

In the context of healing, a trauma doctor Gabor Maté wrote about the Seven A's—Acceptance, Awareness, Anger, Autonomy, Attachment, Assertion, and Affirmation, which offers a holistic approach to emotional and physical well-being. Acceptance helps us face reality without denial; awareness allows us to recognize patterns and triggers. Healthy anger sets boundaries and protects our needs, while autonomy empowers us to make choices true to ourselves. Attachment emphasizes the value of meaningful relationships, assertion encourages expressing our needs confidently, and affirmation reminds us to validate our worth and achievements.

Trust, grief isn't linear, and these stages aren't a checklist—they're a reflection of the emotional journey many of us take during profound loss. Each stage, no matter how difficult, is a step toward healing.

...And, Then I Chose Not To Die!

"We all have two lives, the other one starts when realized when just have one"- Confucius.

A day comes when we realize that the risk of the remaining closet in a bud is greater than the risk of blossom. This means, avoiding risk or holding onto your comfort zone—feels more suffocating than daring to bloom into your full self. Life is certainly a process of becoming, and unbecoming with a combination of states that we go through, people we meet across, and the places we have been into. Life is never about perfection and it's all about randomness.

You don't need to be a compulsive positive thinker rather should express yourself where you should. Health is never a matter of compulsory positive thinking. Rather genuine positive thinking — or, more deeply, positive being — empowers us to know that we have nothing to fear from truth. Molecular researcher Candace Pert highlighted that expressing long-suppressed emotions, like anger, can "jump-start" your immune system. Think of a situation where someone finally shares a deep-seated frustration with a family member. While difficult, the act of voicing those feelings often brings clarity, connection, and a sense of relief.

Not all stories can have a happy ending - yet the wisdom of science, the resilience of the human spirit, and the depth of the soul assure us that no human is ever beyond the reach of renewal. As long as there is life, there is hope for transformation and redemption. The true challenge lies in nurturing that hope—in ourselves and others—and finding ways to support growth, healing, and change. This ongoing pursuit of renewal is not just a question we face but a testament to our shared humanity and enduring potential for reinvention.

"Life is beautiful, crazy, and sometimes silly. And, we humans are amazing. We all know we're going to die one day, but we still keep living. We still get upset over little things, but we keep going, even though time is always moving us closer to the end. We still find joy in simple moments, like a beautiful sunset, the smell of a baby's head, or putting together flat-pack furniture, even though we know everyone we love will eventually be gone. I don't know how we do it, but we do."

I keep reminding myself that life is a bunch of good and bad surprises. It's about finding money in your pocket when you were not expecting it or finding your car with a tyre flat when you were not expecting it too. Well, embrace it, accept it, and absorb it. Begin giving thanks calls amid life, rather than waiting for an ideal moment to do that. Resonate that we may never reach the perfect conclusion we had envisioned, and if we kept ourselves waiting until then to appreciate everything we've been given, that moment of gratitude might never come. So, allow yourself a 'one-more' chance —

Allow yourself to go ahead and take up your space.

Allow yourself to bloom to the fullest.

Allow yourself to dance in the rain.

Allow yourself to laugh as loud as you want.

Allow yourself to dream and fight for that.

Allow yourself to run down the empty streets.

Allow yourself to become a butterfly.

Allow yourself to dare.

Allow yourself to heal.

Importantly, you deserve to be seen, heard, and deeply cared for—not just by others, but by yourself too. You don't have to stay confined in a shell of fear, self-doubt, or societal expectations. Like a caterpillar transforming into a butterfly, your life is meant to be a beautiful adventure full of growth and beauty. It's okay to fail or fall. You spread your wings and embrace the world around you. You deserve joy, love, and freedom, just like everyone else. Take steps, own your life unapologetically, because you matter—your dreams, your voice, and your journey are as valuable and lovable as anyone else's. So, love it, live it.

www.ingramcontent.com/pod-product-compliance
Lightning Source LLC
LaVergne TN
LVHW041935070526
838199LV00051BA/2795